THE JOB OF LIVING

By Stewart Edward White:

Stewart Edward White

THE
JOB OF LIVING

BY
STEWART EDWARD WHITE

Frontispiece

Hickman Systems
New Age Books
4 Woodland Lane
Kirksville, MO   63501

Reprinted 1984

E. P. DUTTON & CO., INC.
PUBLISHERS · 1948 · NEW YORK

TABLE OF CONTENTS

THE JOB
by BADGER CLARK

But God, it won't come right! It won't come right!
I've worked it over till my brain is numb;
The first flash came so bright,
Then more ideas after it—flash! I thought it
Some new constellation men would wonder at.
Perhaps it's just a firework—flash! fizz! Spat!
Then darker darkness and scorched pasteboard and sour smoke.
But, God, the thought was great,
The scheme, the dream—why, till the first charm broke
The thing just built itself, while I, elate,
Laughed and admired it. Then it stuck,
Half done—the lesser half, worse luck!
You see, it's dead as yet: a frame, a body, and the heart.
The soul, the fiery, vital part
To give it life is what I cannot get. I've tried—
You know it—tried to snatch live fire,
And pawed cold ashes. Every spark has died.
It won't come right! I'd drop the thing entire,
Only I can't! I love my job.

You, who ride the thunder,
Do you know what it is to dream and drudge and throb?
I wonder!
Did it come at you with a rush, your dream, your plan?
If so, I know how you began:
Yes, with rapt face and sparkling eyes,
Swinging the hot globe out between the skies,
Marking the new seas with their white beach lines,

THE JOB

Sketching in sun and moon, the lightning and the rains,
Sowing the hills with pines,
Wreathing a rim of purple 'round the plains.
I know you laughed then, as you caught and wrought
The first, swift rapturous outline of your thought.
And then—
Men!

I see it now.
Oh God, forgive my pettish row!
I see your job. While ages crawl,
Your lips take laboring lines, your eyes a sadder light,
For man, the flower and center of it all—
Man won't come right!
After your patient centuries,
Fresh starts, recastings, tired Gethsemanes
And tense Golgothas, he, your central theme,
Is just a jangling echo of your dream.
Grand as the rest may be, he ruins it.

Why don't you quit?
Crumple it all and dream again? But no,
Flaw after flaw, you work it out: revise, refine—
Bondage, brutality and war and woe,
The sot, the fool, the tyrant and the mob—
Dear God, how you must love your job!
Help me, as I love mine.

From: *Sky Lines and Wood Smoke* by Badger Clark.

"This is birth, not death; freedom after bond-age. Gain, not loss; light following after shadow. Tell them not to fear or grieve. He who was afflicted is well again. He who was bound is free."

INVISIBLE.

(*Received by Margaret Cameron.*)

STEWART EDWARD WHITE:

HIS LATER YEARS

A Personal Impression, by MRS. LESLIE F. KIMMELL

STEWART WAS a reticent, even a shy person; yet few people who did not know him well realized that his charm and social poise concealed a deep-seated diffidence. His faculty for keeping silent when nothing needed to be said, and the fact that he was unusually self-contained sometimes caused strangers to feel ill at ease in his presence for a short time. But it was not necessary to be with him long to lose any sense of strain. The very quietness of his manner invited confidence, and his genuine interest encouraged one to talk freely. He was a wonderful listener.

When, after the outstanding success of *The Unobstructed Universe,* letters began to pour in, and later, when many people asked to be allowed to call at his home to talk with him, he was painfully aware of what he felt to be his inadequacy. He had, as he put it, "a holy horror of meddling with other people's inner workings." * But the demand for his counsel could not be ignored. More and more he came to realize that this was his main job. Letters were no problem. He could shut himself away with his ediphone and, quite unself-consciously, dictate replies which were warm and helpful. But personal interviews were a different matter. It had never been easy for him to

* See *The Stars Are Still There,* page 50.

xiii

talk about the things that lay closest to him, even to his inti-
mates; and to discuss prayer, the nature of God, or any other
spiritual matter, with a complete stranger took real courage
on his part. In *The Stars Are Still There* he tells how he would
call for help from Betty before the arrival of a "client." With
the growing realization that he was, indeed, getting support
from the Invisibles, and that by "listening" to them he was
able to say the right thing, his confidence increased, and he
came eventually to enjoy these interviews. He never gave
specific advice, but he did help people to think for themselves,
giving them principles which they could apply to their own
needs.

Always he had the light touch. There was no room in his
philosophy for the lugubrious or the ponderous. The humor
which made him such a popular dinner guest carried over into
every aspect of his life. He loved a good story, and always,
when I arrived for a visit, he would regale me with his latest.
He was charitable in his judgments, not only because he could
put himself in another person's place, but because he could
look upon life so objectively that he treated it more or less
like a drama unfolding before him. But he confessed that this
had not always been his attitude. In his earlier days life had
borne hard on him; he had been critical, easily annoyed, often
sharp in his comments. With the development of his faith in
the authenticity of the teachings that were given to Betty came
a determination to put that philosophy to work, to "make it
so." Gradually, as the years passed, he mellowed, until the
qualities which were so pronounced in his later years re-
placed his earlier austerity. (Who says that one cannot change
after forty!) To me, the opportunity of seeing him put into
practice what he believed, of watching him handle the count-
less small daily trials as well as the more serious problems, and
handle them with poise and humor, was of even greater value

than reading his books. It proved that these teachings really work!

In spite of the fact that many people sought him out for guidance he was no missionary. He never mentioned his psychic work, or that of Betty, unless he was sure that his listener was interested and sympathetic. Always he warned against trying to "convert" people. "You can't go around with a spiritual flit-gun," he would say. "Every fellow has to find his own way. Our approach may not be the one for Mr. X. If he needs it, and when he is ready for it, he will seek it out." And so the many who wanted to found schools or to conduct organized classes to teach Betty's philosophy were gently but determinedly discouraged.

The very human quality of Stewart White's books, and the charm of his letters, have caused many people to wonder what sort of person he was in his daily life. He was besieged with requests to write an autobiography. He invariably replied, "The story of my life is in my books." And so it is, in the main. His African and Alaskan adventures, his experiences in the great West of our own country are to be found in some forty-odd books published before the present series which began with *The Betty Book* and closes with this one.

But readers have wanted to know more about his later years, and especially about the period following Betty's death. Was he in touch with her, except through Joan? Did he, personally, have psychic gifts? This book answers the latter question. Or again, what sort of man was he personally? One of the most noticeable things about Stewart was that he always carried with him the "feel" of the outdoors. His skin was bronzed and ruddy; his eyes had that indescribable expression characteristic of people who are accustomed to scanning the horizon. He saw everything. Even when driving his car, intent on the road ahead, he would note objects which might escape the attention of his passenger. Any movement on the landscape attracted his notice. He used to say that he learned to be on the alert in Africa, where to miss a moving object might cost him his life.

A country walk with Stewart was a delight, for he could identify almost any animal, bird, or wild flower. If, by chance, we came across some specimen unknown to him, he would invent some ridiculous name for it. He had an unusually erect carriage, even for a much younger man, and his quick, lithe step carried him almost soundlessly through the woods or along canyon trails. The Ark, a building adjoining the house at Little Hill, contained mounted trophies of his African trips: a group of lions, the head and tusks of a huge elephant, the leopard which he had choked to death with his bare hands when it attacked a native, a rhinoceros, elands, a hyena, and dozens of other specimens. These were left by his will to the California Academy of Science.

His interest in hunting, however, had long since been transferred from gun to camera. He was an enthusiastic photographer, and the movies which he had taken in his travels and in his own garden delighted guests at Little Hill. After Betty's death it was at once poignant and entertaining to see, in these pictures, her lithe little figure racing along the seashore, or serving tea in the garden.

Stewart was an inveterate and discriminating reader. The mammoth bookshelves in his library contained a medley of volumes on every imaginable subject. He loved poetry which "said something"; and for relaxation he read murder-mysteries, if they were not of the hard-boiled variety. His evenings were usually spent in his library where, seated on a big sofa, a dog curled by his side, he read to the low accompaniment of "background music" from the radio.

Whenever a good movie came to town he would occupy his favorite seat in one of the front loges of the theatre. But he

hated to stand in line at the box office, so he always had a
supply of tickets on hand, bought in advance. "Will you please
tell me," he demanded, "why women stand in line at a box
office, or wait on a corner for a bus, and never get out their
money until the moment arrives to buy their tickets? Do they
like to keep people waiting while they fumble around in their
bags looking for their purses?" I had no answer!

His cairn terriers, Toto and Bibi (Swahili for "Little Boy"
and "Little Girl") were always at his heels. They were beautifully trained, for Stewart did not believe that either children
or animals need be a nuisance. Toto, "the little yellow dog"
which Betty "found" for Stewart shortly after her death, was
a real person; and with him Betty made some of her most amusing demonstrations. Often Toto would sit up opposite an ex-
panse of bare wall looking intently at a spot less than five feet
from the floor (Betty was four feet eleven inches tall), waving
his paws in the way he had been taught to show that they were
"clean" and obviously begging to be played with. Then he
would go through all the motions of retrieving a ball, scuttl-
ing across the room and under furniture, returning with "it" in
his mouth to be tossed again by his invisible companion. Once
the "ball" was thrown through the French doors of the dining
room, and Toto, brought up short by the protecting glass,
peered disconsolately through the pane, and then sat down to
wait for its return.

Life at Little Hill moved in a rhythm which is difficult to
describe, but was definitely felt. Stewart was never a clock
watcher. But he seemed to have been born with a sense of timing which brought him to any appointment, effortlessly, at the
right moment. Tardiness always irked him; and the only
"clients" who ever annoyed him were those who would agree to
arrive at two o'clock only to stroll in unconcernedly at four.
Meals were always served on the dot, and with as much for-
mality as when Betty was here. On a landing of the stairway

stood a beautiful grandfather's clock, brought from Europe many years ago. It had an unusual and convenient accomplishment: one minute after the hour or half hour had struck the chime was repeated. Stewart was vastly amused by the fact that Reider, the butler, always managed to get to the library door to announce dinner just as the second chime sounded. Sometimes we could hear him loitering on the way to make his timing perfect.

This rhythm of living was manifested not only in punctuality but in the pattern of Stewart's days. Each morning he worked at his desk in the Ark, where his study adjoined the trophy room, emerging about 10:30 to garden until noon. During Betty's lifetime her garden was famous for the rare plants which she brought from far places, and which would bloom only for her. After her death they withered and died in spite of every care, although the more hardy varieties flourished in abundance. Because help was scarce during the war, Stewart did all the garden work himself, and was vastly proud of the quantities of vegetables, fruits and flowers which he distributed among his friends.

Gardening finished for the day, and luncheon over, Stewart would somewhat apologetically lie down for an hour. This habit began only in his later years as his strength waned. Then to town for errands, and to the Club for a game of dominoes with "the boys."

Nothing except an untoward event was allowed to interfere with his daily "quiet time" in Betty's Blue-Room. Here, for half an hour, he was shut away from any disturbance, coming out refreshed in body and spirit. Stewart was often conscious of Betty's presence, but never more so than during these meditation hours when she frequently gave him suggestions for a book he might be writing, or help on a question that might be weighing on his mind. Much of the material in *Anchors to Windward* "came through" in this way. I still have in my files the scribbled notes on "Meditation" which he asked me to take down while the impression of what Betty had "said" was still fresh in his mind.

Stewart looked forward eagerly to the time when he could again be with Betty. The one thing he dreaded was prolonged old age or invalidism. Even in his seventies he had the appearance of being much younger. He was virile, vigorous, clear-eyed. "When my time comes," he would sometimes remark, "I hope that I'll be hit on the head and go quickly." Yet, much as he would have welcomed death at any time during the seven years after Betty went, he was determined to carry on his job as long as he was needed. He was convinced that Betty wanted him to further her work in his books and in the ever-increasing contacts with his readers. So his days were filled by a routine which, it was obvious, he had established not only for the purpose of accomplishing his task, but to banish loneliness. No matter how vividly he might feel Betty's presence, the life he had shared with her for so many years was over; the house was big and quiet; the garden missed her magic touch. In speaking of her death he once wrote to me: "No matter how inevitable and valuable the separation may have been in the scheme of things, the fact remains that the loss of the physical presence of so vibrant and exquisite a personality does require, at times, a certain resolution." But in that "resolution" he never faltered.

CHAPTER I.

"Gaelic"

THE WORK that Betty did while she was here, and is doing now that she is in the unobstructed aspect of the universe, is sufficiently set forth in the various books—*The Betty Book, Across the Unknown, The Unobstructed Universe, The Road I Know, Anchors to Windward,* and *The Stars Are Still There.* In the latter two she does not herself appear. They purport to be my own personal products. Nevertheless they actually are part of the whole effort. The material did not come into being in the usual way of authorship—at the desk and as a result of purposed thinking—but piecemeal, a fragment at a time, in the half-hours of formal meditation each day. This type of "communication" was used very briefly and on two occasions only at the time of the Unobstructed Universe divulgence. At the moment of awakening, then, I suddenly found myself in instantaneous possession of a new and completely rounded concept. That could of course be ascribed to action of the subconscious formulating below the threshold of consciousness and then bringing the result to the surface, as probably happens in personal problems or on subjects already under consideration. But these particular concepts seemed more in the nature of the divulgence being given, and we so considered them at the time.

Now lately, as I say, at the end of the "flow-through" period in meditation, that technique seems to have resumed. Again

I suddenly come upon a finished concept, instantaneous and complete. Sometimes it is expressed in actual words; it is as though I had come into possession, all at once, of a printed page. Again its expression is in abbreviated form which requires filling in as to the "connective tissue"—but never change or elaboration in meaning. One reason I am convinced that this is a form of communication is that outside the meditating period the subject—whatever it is—is completely blanked out from my mind. I find it impossible to think about it at all. When I have put it down on paper, that finishes it for me until the next meditation time. Only when all of that particular material has been given, can I see mentally the subject as a whole, and think about it. I seem to come alive to it, as one might say. All this is of interest merely to explain why *Anchors to Windward* and *The Stars Are Still There* are included in the list of Betty's work. And is of value as introduction to what we call the "Gaelic" material.

"Gaelic" was our nickname for what seemed to us a single and definite personality, apparently detailed to tell us what made the wheels go round. The material that came through Betty at that time, by and large, was inspiration, stimulus to growth and expression, with only enough explanation as to mechanics to give direction. Through "Gaelic" our intellectual curiosities were given a certain satisfaction, on the principle that a reasonable measure of knowledge is a buttress to faith. These sessions were rare, and seemed to come only at times when one or another of a certain few people were present and in mental quandary.

This material was given, not through Betty, but through me! Now I did not, and do not, consider myself a "station" as Betty was a station, or as is Joan. For these occasions I think I was what might be called a station by induction. What I mean is that *never did the thing happen unless Betty was present.* I think the phenomenon was an extension, for the moment, of her own mediumship. I am strengthened in this belief by the fact that one other beside myself had the same experience with Betty.*

The mechanics were simple enough, though I do not pretend to understand them. When one or another (or several) of the aforementioned small group was present, and apparently if the thing was desirable, my foot jerked as it does when the knee is hammered in test of reflex action. That was the signal. I bandaged my eyes, lay flat and relaxed. After a moment my usual consciousness seemed to me to sink far down below customary life, there to lie quiescent in a half-somnolent state. Ordinary existence seemed to flow far above me, like the surface of a stream; and I lying in the river bed. Conversation and small happenings in the room sometimes registered on my recognition, and sometimes not. Capriciously so, it seemed to me. For example, I might hear one of the dogs scratching, and that annoyed me; but I might be quite indifferent to the telephone bell and the fact that someone had gone to answer. I heard and understood questions, but I might be only confusedly aware of their purport, or of extended and earnest discussions by those present. I knew that at any moment I could shake off my acquiescence and get up and go about my business: but one of the invariables of this state was that *it never seemed worth while to make just that effort!* I have even determined beforehand that I would do it, for the sake of the experiment: but once at "the bottom of the stream" it became again not worth while, and there I remained until the show was over. I suppose this condition would be called light trance, or half trance, if such labels matter.

While I was in this state a second—or a secondary—personality was released. It functioned up there far above at the surface from which I had sunk. Words and sentences floated down the stream. I recognized them: and pronounced them as

* See Introduction to *With Folded Wings*.

they presented themselves. I did this because I might just as well do it as not. Some flicker of independence assured me that I could stop doing it at any given moment: but again something blanketed me with the feeling that it was not worth while to arouse myself to that inhibition. So invariably I said it, whatever it was.

Now a peculiar part of this performance, as far as I was concerned, was that while I was perfectly aware of what was being presented on the surface so far above my personal consciousness, I was generally so aware of only the fragments immediately above me, so to speak. It was as though I looked up through a tube or tunnel of limited diameter, and could see only what floated directly across it, and for only as long as it remained within that diameter. Sometimes I got only a word or so at a time; more often a phrase; ordinarily a complete sentence or a unit of thought.

As soon as that word or phrase or sentence had floated down stream out of sight—or hearing as the case might be—I had only the most confused recollection of it; nor had I more than the vaguest anticipation of what the next was to be. I doubt if I could have finished any statement merely by the context, for as to context I seemed dulled. Often I have, in my own person, halted a statement to express doubt that it meant anything, or that involved phrases could be brought to a successful conclusion. This doubt was invariably ill-founded. The thing came out all right in spite of me.

Nor, after returning to my normal state, except in a very general way have I ever had any recollection of the detail of the argument. However, if the notes were read to me promptly, I could detect errors and rectify them, or supply words omitted. If the reading was very long delayed, however, the context was strange.

In content these "communications" were quite aside from my habitual trends of thought; often startlingly so. As a professional writer I have, naturally, developed a distinct style of my own. "Gaelic's" style was entirely different. I would be incapable of imitating his manner. I offer no rebuttal to the theory that Gaelic may be a secondary personality of my own, but I myself see no evidence in support of that theory. Nor does it matter. The important point is what is said, not who says it.

CHAPTER II.

Dangerous Doctrines

1.

ORDINARILY TELLING a person what not to do is poor teaching. It is better to affirm, and let the negations take care of themselves. However, sometimes the building site for the projected new structure is so overgrown that a preliminary job of brush clearing is imperative. So we begin with Gaelic by denying the validity of certain concepts that have been forced at us so long that we swallow them whole, without examination. "Without examination" is his crux phrase. He does not throw them overboard, as will later become plain.

We have been taught—and to a certain extent have believed —that there is merit in self-denial, in asceticism.

We pat ourselves on the back for "doing our duty" whether it appeals to us or not.

We have been led to believe that suffering is a powerful agent toward spiritual development.

It could, Gaelic acknowledged, be a dangerous doctrine to preach if we were to deny the validity of these statements. And most certainly assertions to the direct contrary would probably be translated with endorsement of selfishness, self-indulgence and rebellion against personal discomfort. That is why nobody has ventured to make such assertions. However, said Gaelic, I am going to pay you the compliment of considering you "sufficiently advanced to understand," and sufficiently open-minded not to twist things into deliberate misinterpretation. He proceeded to take up these three points in order.

2.

*Asceticism, denial, withdrawal from the world for the sake of spiritual growth is false doctrine.**

The discussion of this was started off by someone's reference to the desirability of "retiring from the ordinary trivialities of ordinary life in order to concentrate more effectively on spiritual growth." He pointed to the admonition of divestment and sacrifice enjoined by many scriptures, including the Bible; and adduced as examples the adepts and saints and holy men who attained by renouncing the world and the flesh.

You have the thing wrong end to, contradicted Gaelic. You seem to think that mere withdrawal and renunciation will make anybody a saint or an adept. But, he pointed out, it is only the adept who can do it! And the latter does not withdraw from life as a means of progress; he withdraws because he has progressed. He does not do so until that is the natural and pleasing thing to him. In seeking growth one expands effort, of course; but the effort should be to expand. Never to contract. To reach out; to gain more contacts; to live everyday life with ever more sympathy. To walk on the highest plane within one's capability. The monastic and wholly mystic is for the rare specialist, not for us. We are here on earth because it gives us the best opportunity for growth. As long as we are here, this is the thing with which we should deal. Earth life must be lived to the full of opportunity, and all that it offers in commonplace everyday living must be used. "If these things are done naturally and simply and eagerly and with a *will*"; said Gaelic, "spirituality, as you call it, will flood in, bringing with it all its gifts of intuition, of spiritual wisdom, of cosmic contact. But that is a thing which must be left to take care of itself. All the other is yours

* See *The Road I Know,* pp. 129-130; *With Folded Wings,* Chap. 5.

to do, and to its doing you bring all that you can of that which comes to you on the flood."

You see, according to Gaelic, the old thesis, "as above, so below," is literally true. No thing, no function, no process of activity here on earth, but has its spiritual complement or counterpart. The full use of the earth phase releases that complementary spiritual content. There is a reciprocity of growth. And naturally, if that is so, negation and denial must be either deterrent or destructive.

Needless to say, such doctrine is no invitation to license. It is perfectly true, as Gaelic says, that "there is no thing, no function, no pleasure, no gratification that cannot express, not only its first and obvious earthly content, but may be made also to release its complementary spiritual content." But we might note the words "may be made." That means we must first find out how, as he further says, "to utilize and educate so that they (our activities) may not only fully and pleasurably express all their earthly capabilities, but also act as conduit to their spiritual counterpart." If the latter is not an ingredient, then we should indeed have only license. "The task of the world is to find and grow into these correspondences." In other words, we get nowhere by mere indulgence.

Per contra we also get nowhere by conscientious and ritualistic giving up of things. Giving things up, per se, has no merit at all. Possibly after we have progressed to a certain point we shall no longer want those particular things, and therefore we shall naturally set them aside. As Betty has said, the grownup does not use a child's toys. But a child is not made to grow up by taking away his toys.

That, he pointed out, is one of the dead ends into which the long spiritual striving of the East has blundered. The Orient has tried to work through negations and avoidances, and as a consequence has fallen into a practical futility as to its own common human welfare. It has attenuated itself into what might be called a sterile and solitary functioning, mostly on a plane not intended in the original plan. It is necessary, then, for evolution to start anew in the richness of the soil.

However the mistake is not peculiar to the Eastern philosophies. It is a human mistake. The West also has made it. Medieval religionism, at its lowest swing, denounced the "earthly" as unspiritual, and emphasized withdrawal and monasticism. For a time anything pleasurable was suspect. We dwelt in a "vale of tears," supportable only because it was the antechamber to future—and unearned—bliss.

"This attitude," said Gaelic, "varied widely in degree, and bore startlingly diverse results. To it is due a great list of prohibitions, ranging from the imposed celibate orders to the keeping of the Sabbath holy by reducing its activities to the smallest trickle that could sustain life. All this diversity could, however, be comprised again in that single dry-rotting word, negation. In place of an expansion to include ever more and more of the multiple functions of material life into their proper expression of their complementary spiritual values, the process tended rather toward a constriction that closed more and more even of those significances already in existence. As a consequence the Western, like the Eastern, philosophy became a product dead-end, without further growth."

The only difference seems to be that the West has begun to shake off that numbing chill of life; the East not yet. That the West has had to do so by going through a materialistic phase is unfortunate, but at least it has begun to move. And the job of development is to continue that movement.

"Your part now," Gaelic said, "is to live, as far as you may, the basic principle of this evolution: that is, to live in full all correspondences that your material earth presents to you; to do so without negation; but so to accept and use each and every one of them that you may eventually discern and knowledgedly attract its spiritual meaning. This is not only a satisfying, but an immensely thrilling pursuit. You exercise in it your instinct and ingenuity, not of your mind but of your heart. And when that complement is finally uncovered by you, sometimes in the most unexpected and unlikely aspects, you will experience an excitement and satisfaction of one who at once discovers and enriches. That use and that meaning are in every natural aspect of your earth life. The future of the general spiritual advance of your race is dependent upon this process. As an individual you contribute your quota of your personal research, for that research is synonymous with growth. In this plowing and fallow time, when it seems the race lives in a muck of materialism, that is the harrowing you may contribute. It is in the muck because it begins a fresh, and we hope more glorious attempt."

The exercise of this principle requires no search for great and noble occasion. The occasion is there in even the most trivial details of life.

"No matter how commonplace, or humble, or apparently wholly earthly it may be," says Gaelic, "nevertheless properly viewed, properly utilized, it can express some aspect of spirit that otherwise could not be as adequately expressed. Until this is attained, in full and appropriate emphasis, that particular development is still in the making.

"The moment you find any philosophy, any system of thought that denies or avoids, you may know that it is wrong. Maybe you will have to search for meanings and adjustments and proportions before your affair will work smoothly, but you cannot cut off part of it and have anything but a monstrosity. That is the trouble with asceticisms. The idea is not to divest yourself, but to utilize yourself, to express the whole of yourself, and not just a part.

"The ultimate aim, for method, in the highest utilization of any such material environment as your earth, is the fullest expression of spirit in the completest manifestation of matter.

"The balancing," said he, "is the art of life. The ascetic is no more praiseworthy than the sensualist, and the sensualist is no more to be blamed than is the ascetic. And the pure intellectual is no more admirable—or deplorable—than either."

So much for asceticism and negation.

3.

Self-sacrifice, per se, for its own sake, is false doctrine.

It is popularly supposed to have great power in spiritual development. The principle is all right, but its nature and application are most often misconceived. Many teachings insist on the sacrifice of oneself for others as a counsel of perfection. We give lip-acquiescence to the idea that we should yield ourselves for others, and yet at the same time we have a vague contempt for the mild, meek, kick-me type. Is this recoil a false instinct?

Gaelic maintains it is, on the contrary, most sound. Self-sacrifice of the true sort, and when indicated, is all right, but indiscriminate self-sacrifice for its own sake—and for the feeling of virtue it can be made to bring—is all wrong. "Indeed," says he, "it is often merely an indication of laziness or of a vain self-righteousness. In true self-sacrifice a man gives up something which is ordinarily and naturally an object of desire, not because of some rigid intellectual idea of duty, nor because of some weak sentiment or emotion, nor because of some mistaken conception that stripping himself to present to others is a meritorious thing in itself; but because the extension of his inner nucleus of complete knowledge has made him aware that the occasion demands, for the harmony of which he is a part, a foregoing rather than an insistence. It then becomes a natural process," he adds, "and in final analysis a joyous process, as is any harmonious functioning." As the world ordinarily uses the term, sacrifice implies deprivation with pain and regret. In that sense there is here no sacrifice at all.

"Indeed," suggested Gaelic pertinently, "if there is pain or regret, it is likely that the sacrifice is not justified! Even if a man has to struggle with himself to arrive at the point of relinquishment, having arrived there, the test is whether through his intellectual decision he experiences a completely unregretful satisfaction and a sense of having done the totally harmonious thing. If still there lingers a strong sense of mere duty, that in itself is an indication that he has not functioned entirely within his field of complete self-knowledge."

It is not a matter of "facing one's duty" at all, says Gaelic. Even if, from a purely objective viewpoint, a man "should" make the sacrifice, his first struggle should not be directed toward giving the thing up. It should be within himself, to extend the boundaries of his self-awareness, until he *wants* to give the thing up. Not because the thing is less desirable to keep; but because that is the way he really feels about it. Only when such inner satisfaction coincides with his intellectual duty-decision should he go ahead.

"Besides," pointed out Gaelic, "it may well be that his duty-decision is intrinsically wrong, though he may not know it." Knowingly to abandon to others that which is not their right and that which they should themselves earn, says Gaelic, in effect, deprives you both of opportunity for growth. Just because someone asks us to do a thing is *in itself* no reason why we should do it. Nor does the fact that a crying need comes within the orbit of our notice *in itself* impose an obligation on us.

"The situation must be evaluated from your consciousness of what is within yourself," says Gaelic, rather than by what seems to be another's need. "The latter you cannot judge in all its implications." We have not the wisdom to understand what the real need may be. "You may," warned Gaelic, "even do harm by frustrating or deflecting a lesson of experience."

4.

Doing our duty is not always meritorious.

In his clearing the underbrush by these various negations of "dangerous doctrine" Gaelic went even further. Just as what we call self-sacrifice is often unwarranted, so what we call selfishness is often temporarily useful for the long run. The phrase "what we call" should be borne in mind.

"Your first duty in development is the homogeneous, close-knit invulnerable core of yourself as an individual."

Parenthetically, the fact that this "primary central establishment" is an indispensable and must be built and assured before one is justified in trying to go ahead further, is one reason why development is sometimes so slow.

"It is—no matter how small the scale—, the first step, the indispensable step, in the creation of the eternal self. And it must be done: whether it takes a decade, a half-century, a whole life-time, or the repeated incarnations of a number of phases. *No further forward movement can safely, effectively or constructively be attempted until this is accomplished.* The occupation of wider and richer area toward your ever unknown boundaries can proceed only after this fact."

Gaelic could not be too emphatic in his insistence on this. No use trying to be noble until you have something to be noble with!

"Therefore," says he, "stop until the assurance is gained, no matter what the implication your course may seem to have of self-centeredness."

Which of course does not mean self-centered use of what we do possess. This is no doctrine of egocentricity.

"But," and Gaelic paused impressively as though to lend weight to what he was about to say, "—and here is a truth so profound that I would have it in a separate paragraph:

"Outgiving is never constructively effective unless it is an overflow."

Of course, he admitted, you can give out something, by pumping up in response to "what is expected" or what is "the proper thing," or what you are persuaded is "your obligation to the world." But pumping up means always depletion; depletion means vacuum, and vacuum is a vortex of attraction for that which your own processes have not created. Overflow, on the other hand, is a super-abundance that leaves no lack behind it, but still the filled reservoir of accomplishment. When you rush forth to give, driven by your natural instincts of sympathy, or desire to re-construct, or sensitivity to conditions, pause to consider whether you are leaving your territory unoccupied, open to an invasion that ultimately is going to make you ineffective. Your place as a component part of the greater whole is primarily yourself and only secondarily that which you accomplish outside yourself. That the "secondarily" may be important is acknowledged, *but it is impossible* that it should be aught but ephemeral if the "primarily" is not a solid reality. In this sense it is your *business* to be selfish, in the shining aspect of that word, and the great paradox is that the shining use of selfishness enables you to be effectively, and without disintegration, what the world calls "unselfish."

"Keep in mind," he thought it important enough to repeat, "that only from overflow of abundance can you give effective help. If the abundance is not yet gained, in the particular respect in which the demand is apparently made, then an attempt to supply from depletion will result only in harm to the both of you. But be sure of one thing," he added, "that the genuine overflow of that which is abundant within you can never harm.

"I advise you," he added, "to re-examine certain old saws that a self-seeking age has warped to its own ends. 'Charity begins at home' is one of them. That means merely the assurance of overflow rather than depletion."

It is fatal to stop half-way. The real meaning of duty lies in the obligation of using overflow once we have gained to it.

The wrong kind of doing our duty Gaelic stigmatized as "drab-colored duty." He doubted the value of anything done without zest. Indeed he seemed to question the permanence of anything that lacked this important ingredient; as though one were to mix cement without sand. "Whatever," he says, "has been done with love endures, either in the physical world, in the spiritual contacts, in human relations, or in the substance of thought. All else is consumed. The word *love*," he hastened to add, "has become a palimpsest overlaid with the scribblings of many, until the simple original has been obscured. If I were to attempt, in a word, to define what I mean, I would say *things done heartily*. Those alone have complete and ultimate influence."

Sometimes he humorously considered whether the word duty ought to have any standing with us at all.

"It might even be doubted whether one *should* 'do his duty' when it appears to him with a capital D," said he. Not unless, he qualified, he can go back to it and discover something inclusive of it which he can perform heartily. So that the distasteful duty with the capital D turns out to be only one detail of a scheme that is not distasteful at all. Then Gaelic dropped his facetiousness.

"I speak here, of course, as you well understand, in a rather exaggerated hyperbole," he reminded. "It is sometimes desirable to do certain drudgeries which cannot be avoided, pending the discovery of the leaven which will make them palatable. Such performances are often valuable, as calisthenics, in strengthening spiritual muscles. But one does not thereby attain grace, as so many worth-while people imagine. In no *direct* sense is the disagreeable constructive. Otherwise one could gain grace by brushing his teeth with brown soap."

From this point of view Gaelic saw the so-called "revolt" of the new generation (this was in 1925) as a good thing, in principle.

"A very healthy rebellion—the younger generation overturning our lifeless idols of duty and sacrifice and such things. What they have not discovered yet—life will surely teach them —is the seeing of the scheme of responsibility whole. That will finally reveal, in their essential structure, duty and sacrifice as full-blooded essentials of conquest, rather than old dried mummeries of dogma."

5.

Pain and suffering are necessary to development.

This is the final bit of underbrush to be cleared.

"We must suffer to learn," one of us remarked bromidically. Gaelic pounced on this.

"That persistent misconception has grown up in your body of thought," said he. "You have given suffering a therapeutic value of its own. You have conceived that, in some vague and mysterious manner, suffering has in itself a power of developing. Your body of thought is full of phrases indicating this, which may all be epitomized in one: 'he was developed by suffering.' In your body of thought you have also another phrase which has become part of your legend, epitomized in this quotation: 'he was brutalized by his suffering.' But strangely enough you have never thought to place these two phrases in juxtaposition, to examine them together.

"Understand directly, there is nothing whatever in this. Suffering fulfills one function only in 〔obscured〕uction. It sensitizes the surface for the reception of the impress. The final effect depends entirely upon what impression is made upon that sensitized surface. It is available for impression only by yourself, and will receive and record only what you knowledgedly bring to it, or that which you are too careless or too ignorant to fend from it. A period of suffering is a fertile time; but fertile for what? One of the great spiritual sins is a smug complacence in suffering, that sits back in a purring pride of confidence that this mere endurance *must* result in an otherwise unearned heavenly crown.

"A period of suffering, then, is only an opportunity to utilize that which a happier period has constructed or acquired. Only if it is so utilized has it any developmental efficiency. To sit back in expectation of reward for being a martyr is a vain proceeding."

Times of turmoil in the world, said he, follow exactly the same law and can be subjected to the same analysis. They have no direct developmental effect. They offer sensitization to whatever is brought to them.

6.

The basic trouble back of all these mistakes of partial thinking lies in the fact that we are trying to deal in ultimates. We are not ourselves ultimates, and until in the course of evolution we so become, we cannot do so. The ultimate of cosmos is harmony. We comprehend that intellectually, and so we deny the actuality of evil. The ultimate of physics is pure force, and so we deny the reality of matter. And on the basis of these denials we build logical structures of thought by which we attempt to deal with the intermediates of health and disease and sin by calling them error; with the pressure of economics by leaping the intermediate of human nature as it is to an ultimate of altruism; with the solidities of natural environment by dissolving them into the mechanism of illusion rather than getting out our monkey wrenches and fixing the machine. And so futility. We are intermediates in evolution; we live in the intermediate; with intermediates we must deal, whatever our realization that the ultimate exists.

CHAPTER III.

From Illusion to Reality

1.

WHAT THE brush-clearing really boiled down to in positive statement was simply this: that here, on this earth and in the life we are supposed to live, spiritual values cannot express themselves except through the material. And, per contra, if we are to deal with the spiritual at all, we must do so through and by means of the hard solid world-facts which are our environment.

It is possible to by-pass the material and get some sort of result. But success achieved by such direct dealing is one alien to our present field of action. It bears no relationship. It is as though one were to try to raise tropical orchids in a north-country potato patch. Better stick to the potatoes, especially if potatoes are really our job. Later we may have another job, to do with orchids; but right now we are embedded in the material and with the material we have to deal. Then let us not try to dodge that fact, but rather accept it heartily, at the same time striving to discover and express its spiritual complement. To learn how to do that is one of the reasons why we are here on earth at all.

The only way to do so is to live, and to function, right here and now, and in the manner of our environment.

2.

Things, says Gaelic, may be symbols of reality; or actually containers of reality. When in simple static relationship to one another—in other words, when they are not functioning—they are symbols. They merely stand for something, as a note on a page stands for a musical sound. But when they begin to function, then they become containers of reality. This is a general rule, and mankind is no exception to it.

All by himself, without functioning in any fashion with the outside world, a man's only reality is himself. He to himself is not a symbol. Things outside himself remain merely symbols of possibilities until he acts with them. They stand for, but do not embody. In them he may surmise the existence of realities, and by their aid as symbols he may gain some degree of critical understanding of their realities. "But," these are Gaelic's words, "they will touch him only as a shadow touches the wall, leaving no impress." They give him no experience of solid fact, *and experience is a major and necessary ingredient of growth.* His only experience of solid fact is confined to himself. The point at first seems a trifle obscure, but it will clarify.

Nevertheless, he possesses a core of reality in himself, and from that he can expand when, and only when, he turns to outside functioning, to living. He is real to himself because in himself is the ingredient of reality, the functioning. There is nothing mystic or occult in the idea. Gaelic expresses it thus:

"His appetites, his emotions, his passions, his imaginations, the coursing of his blood through his veins, the registration of light through his eyes, his movements, and every activity which is his, are not to him symbols, but are expressions of that which is his inner self, seeking outlet in a world of movement. The living intangibles flow through their respective mechanisms within him to produce, as far as his consciousness is concerned, a portion, limited though it may be, of absolute reality."

But as long as he remains thus self-contained, within himself, he exists in what amounts to a dream world in which all things are to him symbolical—except himself. "So true is this," says Gaelic, "that certain ones who are by nature contemplative and externally almost non-active, have gravely propounded as a philosophical system that the external world is illusion, a fine-spun absurdity of subjectivists. Such a man lives actually, however he rationalizes himself, in a world of poetry, whose substance is that of dreams and whose endurance is as fleeting. If he is of mystic quality he is perpetually in anticipation of some remote time or state of existence when he shall break down the *veil of illusion,* as he calls it, to an undefined and rather vague reality of an unguessed form which he imagines to lie behind."

"You can be told no new thing," Gaelic emphasized the principle. "You can be told the words, but you will not understand them. Action is all of development. The very first slight wee crawly movement on the part of the most microscopic creature you can discern is an action whose first reason is, not existence or insurance of the means for existence, but development-action. Any new thing must be acquired by experience in action before it can be told, either by you to yourself or by you to someone else. Hence the vagueness and the gropings and the dissatisfactions of the approach to any new thing. You must first confront it, become aware that it exists. It is something— just something. You cannot understand, because you have no experience. Then you must act; and from the act and its result you have knowledge. For that reason you can never see clearly ahead of your experience."

The escape from this "illusion of illusion" is simple. A thing ceases to be merely a symbol of reality and becomes a container of and an embodiment of reality when it functions in relationship to something else. So the moment a man stirs about into such a relationship, things cease to be merely symbols—"illusions"—and become solid facts. And as he is able to stir about

and do, to that extent he removes things from the category of
symbols *suggesting* truth into the category of actualities *con-
ducting* truth.

That is the Job: to fashion skills, understandings, abilities,
tools to function in ever wider inclusion of his environment.

It is indispensable. We cannot skip a step.

"It is impossible to function safely in advance without a
foundation of complete functioning in the plane of life in which
one is placed," said Gaelic. "Those few who safely have attained
in your earth life and elsewhere have done so on a foundation of
complete earth function. This is an invariable rule and an indispensable safeguard. Life in advance is a blossoming on firm
earth roots. Perception in advance is a true perception only
when it is a growth from complete earth living. All other perception is partial and veiled with the phantasms of illusion."

3.

But perfecting our skills and ourselves as tools is only one part
of the job. We may be remarkably successful at that and still
not have arrived much of anywhere. Through functioning we
develop—to an extent—"skills, understandings, abilities, tools."
We are not privileged to sit down and admire that as a final
accomplishment. "The penalty for the fashioning of a tool is
that it must be used or it will rust," says Gaelic. "The obligation
of having developed correspondences, aptitudes, talents, skills,
techniques is their employment." Through the process of their
fashioning, to be sure, we have infused living reality into what
has heretofore been symbol. But if we would keep it real we
must continue the process. Neglect to do so "blunts the perception so that, in time, that particular thing will cease, not only
to be a conductor of truth, but even to symbolize. And so it will
end at last in something lifeless, useless—and dead things must
be painfully carried away."

We must use what we have. And also it is well to realize what we have.

"On reaching mature years," mused Gaelic, "it should be, and it will be in time, a spiritual requirement that each man should sit down with himself to take stock of his equipment. He must examine to see what he has learned to do in the matter of this transmutation; for what he has learned to do cries out for its fulfillment. He has called to life a need of fulfillment of reality which did not exist before. He has to an extent chosen a road which in some way or another he must tread out; or, if not precisely a road, he has taken a direction. The path his feet may tread may not be precisely that which he had in view when he started, but his ability to function must be in some way fulfilled. He must lay his aptitude and talents, and the rest, before him as on a table, and he must say to himself: 'These things are mine, they are in my possession, and in some degree I am skilled in their use. Furthermore, in one way or another I must use them. They are the obligation of my equipment in this life. I may not use them in the way I intended when I fashioned them, but of them some use I *must* make. Otherwise the reality I have called close to me will, in its nature, recede, and about me will deepen and darken the veil I have so sore labored to thin.' Mankind is prone to greediness and, like a child, would grasp ever more than his hands can hold." The very fashioning of the tool creates an obligation for its use. Its owner is justified in abandoning it only when through some other aptitude he is able to perform the same function of transmutation.

"Now," warned Gaelic with a touch of humor, "beware lest too close inspection of a very large and general law gets you to splitting hairs of literal interpretation. There is, of course, room for experiment and room for expanding in new interests."

Nor are we to apply the obligation so rigidly that we shall keep right on doing it—whatever it is—merely because we have made the tool.

When I speak of obligation, said Gaelic, it is merely "an effort to show you that it is not only desirable, but the law, that one should choose. And that, once having chosen, he should maintain his greater directions. It is to discourage too great a scattering of forces, and too ready a tendency to stop short on the path.

"The obligation to function is not so onerous as you might fear," he interpolated, as an aside. "Developed muscles require less exercise than those in the building. Accustomed action takes less attention than the learning.

"And the first choice may be a mistaken one," he resumed the thread of argument. "It is not a fatal and divorceless marriage. But it is well to analyze very carefully—or, oftener, to test by the feeling of the unsatisfied equation within—that it is mistaken. And the old should not be abandoned until an equal transmutation of reality is assured in some other direction." Mistakes do little harm, if they are honest, and if they are honestly abandoned when so recognized. "Genuine mistakes very rarely result in a very high transmutation," Gaelic assured us. What he was trying to get over, he told us, was that, though we may abandon mistakes with profit and a clear conscience, we should guard against quitting an activity of function because of whim or without sufficient cause.

Gaelic realized apparently that his thesis could be questioned and shot full of dialectic holes, but he insisted on it as a basis for his future talks.

"This evening," he acknowledged, "is a crude, rough, and general statement. If you dissect it in detail with your intellectual scissors and forceps, you will probably find much to question and perhaps to deny. That is due to the fact that a complete statement is impossible for a great variety of reasons. But if the general principle is laid away in some absorptive corner of your spirit, it will cause you to grow into a fuller understanding than I can at present express. Plant it and water it;—do not pick it to pieces, for I cannot myself tell from here how much or how little of that particular reality I have functioned into you."

4.

At the time, and as far as we were concerned, Gaelic's deprecation was unwarranted. We accepted the hypothesis and went on from there. One of our discussions was as to "living through" an experience. "I've lived through all that completely," was the argument. "I've surrounded it. I've got all there is to be got out of that kind of experience. There is no sense in going on repeating it endlessly. That faculty I can now discard. Repetition is nothing but drudgery after it becomes rote."

Were not these "functioning faculties" of Gaelic's in the same category? Once a faculty had been perfected, and then utilized to its limit, should not one discard its further use? Or at least be justified in so doing? Perhaps that thought tied in with the renunciations urged by many spiritual teachings: get rid of everything "worldly" from meat to sex.

There are two reasons why not, said Gaelic. The first is that faculties are developed not only to furnish you experience through their functioning, but to bring you in touch with reality through the real-izing of symbol. That he had explained in his original hypothesis.

"We can best understand the second reason by considering some faculty actually outgrown and abandoned.

"To avoid all possibility of dispute we would best take for our example something in the physical organism, as for instance the vermiform appendix. This at one time subserved a useful and indispensable purpose in that it formed a large by-pass reservoir for the breaking-up and the bacillar inoculation of the food which the animal organism at that stage of its development ingested. In other words, crude though the process was, through function the grasses and herbages, which to primitive intelligence could be naught but vague symbols of hunger-satisfying possibilities, became life-bestowing reality.

"In the course of evolution, that which we might call 'appendix faculty' was 'lived through,' in your definition, and abandoned. In your reasoning the possessing entity had from that particular faculty extracted all the experience it could bestow, and was therefore impelled to move on to the construction and occupation of higher faculties.

"But, be it noted that the error in this reasoning here becomes plainly evident. Before the old faculty even began its process of atrophy, a new faculty—the later chemistry of the intestinal tract—had been fully developed and in function. A novel apparatus had come into existence fully capable of transmuting at least an equal amount of symbolism into reality—or grass into energy—and probably in much larger quantity. The abandonment of the old was not conditioned on the fullness of experience acquired through its functioning, but solely on the fact that a replacing and higher faculty was fully completed to take its place."

So, he pointed out, we see development going on in a twofold rhythm. We use, heartily, whatever attributes and free functioning faculties we possess. By that means we take part in the transmutation of the great world about us. At the same time, by that very activity, we are slowly evolving new attributes and faculties, which in due time will be ready to function. When they are fully ready to function, they will supersede that which is outgrown.

"But until that time is reached,"—Gaelic was emphatic—"the obligation of hearty and eager and vivid and complete activity of the old faculties and powers, utilized on the material most appropriate to them, is the most necessary, if not the most important, obligation of existence."

We all know the type of fellow, Gaelic reminded us, who is a sincere and laborious aspirant to spiritual advancement;

but who, in spite of his dedicated life, is restless, baffled, uncomfortable, or even wholly unhappy. "He is," said Gaelic quaintly, "trying to get along without his appendix before he has developed a stomach." Man's usefulness in the present lies in functioning with what he has. By that means, and by that means only, he fulfills his spiritual relationships in transmuting appearance, the symbol, into reality. That is his first obligation. He is not privileged to develop new powers, if that development is at the expense of his present legitimate activity. Nor if it is for use in an environment beyond his present state. Nor in advance of his possibility of present use.

Gaelic did not wish to be misunderstood as to this point. Function and use, as he used the terms, were not intended to discourage exploration, reaching out in advance. Functioning of one's present equipment is only a part of normal activity. Groping ahead is another. The emphasis, however, is on the first. The balance, in proportion, must be maintained.

CHAPTER IV.

Groups

1.

In all this preliminary brush clearing and definition of the Job, Gaelic had been considering the individual as a single unit. This, he now implied, had been merely a matter of convenience, much as we compartment off our mental equipment into subconscious, conscious and superconscious. They are of course not actually three separate things. So the individual is not a solitary plant, to be treated and cultivated singly. He has interrelations. Whatever job he does, must be done with reference to those interrelations.

We must work with people. Cooperate.

Work done effectively is through the traits and powers we share. In the common denominator, in other words.

Therefore we work best with and through those with whom we are in affinity. We may be in almost exact alignment with one other person; a little less so with two; and still less as numbers increase. Of necessity the larger the group, the lower the common denominator. For certain simple and direct purposes the common denominator of enormous bodies of men is high enough to do the job. A whole nation can cooperate appropriately for certain things. Or, again, we make the mistake of enlisting a multitude to a problem which, by its very nature, requires higher faculties than can possibly be a common denominator to so many. Cooperation then becomes indiscriminate, and futile. Too often a worthy cause is besmirched and bewildered by over-eager organization into clubs, societies, movements.

Any group, for any purpose whatever, should be assembled and held together by the affinity of its members to the job to be done. Whether or not, outside that job, they are individually in affinity, is a secondary matter. That has nothing to do with the reason for the group.

We are talking here of formal organizations, deliberately planned, for specific purposes—clubs, associations, societies, unions—that sort of thing. They are usually formed to do something too big for one person to handle.

Also, Gaelic pointed out, we belong, by birth, chance or choice to another set of groups. At the simplest we are one of a family. And progressively of a tribe, a nation, a race. And finally of humanity itself. From some of them we cannot escape. We cannot quit being men. We are irretrievably Chinese, if we were born in China. As to some others we have a certain choice. We can naturalize as Americans, if so be it we prefer America to our native country. We can go forth to seek our fortune, out of the family circle, when we come of age.

But whether the group is consciously organized or not, the basic principle remains the same.

"Any group of people," insists Gaelic, "no matter how large or how small, is a group because of a certain impetus in the world for the working out of which to its finish of dynamics the contribution of effort of a single individual is not sufficient. The impetus is at once a product of, and a responsibility of, a certain group type of entity. When that impetus is worked out, whether it be of constructive or deterrent or destructive nature, that group, whether it be of a single family, a nation, or a race, dissolves and comes to an end."

You and I are in our groups for the simple reason that that is where we belong! We are enlisted in them, often, by force of our equipment, our degree in evolution, even our limitations! Because, in short, we are the sort of persons we are.

So there is no sense in resenting our situation as "unjust," "not in any way our fault."

If rebellion only is our attitude, we shall get nowhere; and as far as we are concerned, our group will get nowhere. When we sulk in our tents we are withholding what we are here to contribute. The more malingering there is, by any members of the group, the longer the postponement of its dissolution. The group dissolves, remember, only when the job that draws it together is done. So, if we want to get rid of those conditions that irk us as unjust, it is a good idea to buckle in. We must get rid of the let-George-do-it idea.

Letting George do it is poor business. If George happens not to feel like doing it "that thing, in the group impetus," says Gaelic, "remains still undone. It remains to be done, and must now await another combination of circumstances making that thing possible. That may not recur until after a considerable time, and the group is burdened with the effects until that time has come."

Nor, it seems, have we got out of anything ourselves, presumably. If George does do it, we must pay him back.

"In the law of compensation sooner or later you must make restitution in kind for whatever you have appropriated. Some time in your two histories an extra effort from yourself for the other will be demanded and must be made, when condition and opportunity serve. This apparently gratuitous service accounts for most of the responsibility for others outside of the natural affection and desire. It is an affinity which you will probably recognize."

"How," asked one of us, "do you know when you owe such service?"

"That is a very pertinent question," replied Gaelic. "The gratuitous service that one owes comes about in such a way, when the conditions are ripe, that one is forced to pay it by force of circumstance."

Gaelic added another interesting item to this admittedly obscure complication. The probability is that we shall make good what George supplied for us, not in his coin, but in our own. In other words, repayment is rarely direct.

"It is difficult to make this clear by illustration," admitted Gaelic. "But you are not to rush to a neighbor's plot to do yourself what he has not done. You stay on your own plot and absorb the disharmony of his neglect by constructing another harmony of your own, perhaps wholly different in kind, to fill out the measure. If, in the large inclusion of all mankind, he who dwells on one side of the globe would do his share in absorbing the destructive forces loosed by war on the other side of the globe, he should not do so by going to that war and 'fighting for the right,' but he should rather do something at home, like building a bridge; for in the particular manifestation of bridge, or dam, or road, or spiritual labor, or brotherliness is released the *essence* of constructive harmony. And each such contribution adds its bit toward overmatching the *essence* of destructive disharmony released by avoidance of responsibilities in the great interwoven pattern.*

"The ultimate blending in final harmony with larger cosmic currents," epitomized Gaelic, "may be hastened or delayed according as the members of the group accept and work out those group tendencies or characteristics, which at first view seem sometimes unjust, sometimes unaccountable, and always outside any dependencies, so far as we can see, on anything the individual is or desires or has done."

In short—Gaelic considered the principle important enough to repeat—"If he finds himself hampered and confined in any

---

* Gaelic was then referring to wars in which we are not personally involved except in our sympathies. The Second World War was then some years away.

way by anything outside any impetus which he himself has originated, whether that limitation is by accident of body structure, of temperament, of overwhelming group tradition imposed on him in his plastic youth, he must reflect that this is the condition of his group problem, it is the field of his group activity, it is his opportunity of group contribution, quite aside from his intimate, entirely personal job. He must reflect that he is allied to this group and imposed upon by these conditions because, in a way too complicated to sketch here, his own problem, his own degree in development, fits him to it—just as his other characteristics drew him magnetically to clothe himself in those confining physical characteristics which we call heredity. And he must reflect, for his encouragement, that each hampering or confining group-characteristic which he succeeds, through his own personal development, in lifting from its lower turmoil to conscious higher harmony, is that much done and finished with and put behind of the whole group problem."

2.

All this, Gaelic acknowledged, may seem highly theoretical and a little confusing. It clarifies if we confine our attention for the moment to the smallest and most obvious group inclusion, the family. It is not by chance, says Gaelic, that we are subjected to the advantages and restrictions of this set of blood relatives or that. There exists the magnetic attraction—on both sides—of needs. The kind of person I am can be of assistance in the job of that particular group: that group, and its problems, is the one most capable of helping me, peculiarly constituted as I am.

Groups may be in affinity, drawn together for constructive as well as destructive reasons. That goes without saying. But for the moment Gaelic is dealing with the latter. So now he assumes a family "with a tremendous black burden of narrowness, bigotry, intolerance—whatever you will." These are what we call "family traits." If the members carry on that tradition generation after generation it will grow in power and volume and influence, until an inharmony is created in cosmos of tremendous consequences. And it will persist as a deterrent thing to which human entities will be magnetically drawn, until bit by bit and little by little through hard-won illumination those individuals have lived out and through to harmony, and little by little and bit by bit have dissolved it."

Now a child born into that family, in his earlier years, falls into the prevailing attitudes. It is merely following out a well-known and acknowledged biological law. As an embryo maturing toward birth it has passed swiftly through all the phases of physical evolution, in that it has been successively germ, amoeba-like creature, reptile, fish, tailed beast and so on up to its final form. So now, before his maturity into independent grown-up action, it is quite in order that he pass through, in his personal growth, the spiritual development that has brought his family to what it is. As a young child he has all the family habits, family outlooks, ideas, and prejudices. He heartily endorses the family's loves and hates, its tastes, its religion, its politics. He considers wholly admirable sympathy or hardness, courtesy or rudeness, gentleness or violence according to which is the family atmosphere. We do not blame the child for that. Only when he grows up to an age when he should "commence to think for himself" do we begin to expect from him a little independence. And even then we are inclined to make certain allowances "for his bringing up."

"We do not always hold a child responsible for storming at the servants. It is the family habit, and he thinks it is the only way. The man who has literally never realized cannot be responsible for what he does not know. But intellect and the perceptions come into contacts outside the group, and they cannot fail to bring the seeds of enlightenment through comparison."

But when he has caught up to date, so to speak, we are justified in hoping from him a little discrimination. He ought to begin to see with some objectivity. "He ought to be getting to the point where he can begin to modify, to resolve the family temper or the family pride, the family point of view toward human kind, the family religion and the family politics, the family traits of all kinds that make that group."

The period of his blind loyalty should be past. He is at a cross roads. "He does one of two things: he controls and utilizes them by the alchemy of his personality; or he continues unresisting their tradition."

That is where the group *may* make for loyalty.

"Yes, Uncle Peter is a hard, dour man," said Gaelic drily. "He oppresses the poor and steals from the rich. He will probably be hanged at last. But he is in the family. Let us get together and work it out, so that there will not be another embodiment of another Uncle Peter! For, just as long as his problem remains unsolved, it must continue to seek embodiment in the family. Perhaps it is *your* particular job to rid the family of Uncle Peterishness. If you succumb and carry on the Uncle Peter tradition, so to speak, then you impose a burden on another who is to come. And you do not release yourself from *any part* of the job; you must still, *here or elsewhere,* bend your back to that labor."

3.

Possibly it is unnecessary to warn that we do not go around like knights-errant priggishly jousting at Uncle Peter. Our contribution is rarely—perhaps never—deliberate reform. It is doing our own personal job, with an eye out to avoid or nullify such handicaps as our group may impose. Our personal problem is also the group problem. That is one reason we belong to the group. "Therefore," says Gaelic, "if a man works out his individual development, he automatically also works

out, as far as the individual can, the group problem. It follows
that if the group problem is by so much carried out, there is
so much less of it to weigh upon the other members of his
group. In that thought you may glimpse the interrelations of
effort, and the value to others of that real progress you make
for yourself. You may also, perhaps, glimpse the reverse, and
perceive how imposing additional limitations on yourself
through inertia and indifference imposes an additional burden
of limitations on those magnetically attracted to your group.
Responsibility, in the case of such a man, has been passed
on and must be worked out by others who follow. Furthermore
he has by his indifference so accentuated those certain qualities
in himself that his magnetic attraction toward this type of limitation in the future is greatly intensified." He will have more of
the same in the future!

So, says Gaelic, we may as well accept our limitations,
whether they are personal, or group; and we may as well do so
in welcome rather than resentment. At least, he points out, we
may find encouragement in the thought that after all "degree
of development is not measured by space passed but by pressure overcome," and that here we may "find opportunity for
exerting pressure which would not otherwise be afforded. The
measure of one's life from this point of view," he adds, "must
be, not only one's personal progress but also to what degree one
has emerged—constructively—from the undiluted group attitude of his youth into an individual solution." And, of course,
he reminded us, we get from our group—whatever it is—help
as well as handicap. We come into powers and command of
aid that are beyond our lone strength; and of the group loyalty
which is the basis of family cohesion, of race patriotism, of
finishing the job! And we possess the comfort of backing, so
that we have the right to call upon that combined power. We
have that right because we ourselves shall be called upon to
do only that which is within our capacity of achievement.

Balancing it up, says Gaelic quaintly, one may well say of those conditions which we have resented as personal injustice, "This disagreeable has come to me. It does not matter whether it is through my own fault or the deficiency of another the burden of which I am to assume; or whether it is from the blended deficiencies of that in cosmos which is claiming my relationship," and let it go at that.

Above all we must not dodge the issue on the argument that, since it is not our personal fault, it is none of our affair. Avoidances are very bad business indeed. Not only do we fail to get out of anything thereby, but we have actually added to the group burden. Someone must do our share for us. And since the group burden is also our burden, sometime or other we shall have to repay that loan, probably in less favorable circumstances. Better face it, and get at it, and get it over with.

Furthermore Gaelic proceeded to rub it in by a hypothetical and horrible example. Remember that avoidance is not merely a postponement. It results in a definite narrowing of powers. The second chance, when it comes along, is even more difficult to face, for the reason that we are now less adequate to it. If we could imagine a man who persisted in avoidance until it became a habit, we would shortly find him so narrowed down by it, and at the same time so held to that same sort of thing, which must be done, that "when near the vanishing point of this continued process he would be narrowed, not only to the point of such physical disability as cripples him to a place of contemplation in the sun, but his mental movements bound within the circumference of almost the lowest animal."

We would have then a moron, or an imbecile, incapable of helping himself, overwhelmed by his limitations of body or mind. If he is to emerge from this state, he must be helped. If it were not for his group, he would be lost.

"For," says Gaelic, "there comes a time when movement seems to hang in a balance of equilibrium, and it is a question whether or not the germ of personality is to dissolve into its original elements, or swing back up the slow and difficult arc. At that point it seems that even the opportunity for exerting what you call proportionate pressure has left the power of that atrophied will. Some outside help must be given, not toward supplying a deficiency which the entity itself must fill for stable development, but merely to place it in the way of making the first effort."

That is where the group comes in, the group which he himself has failed. He must belong to *some* group, even if it is so broad a one as the human race. And the human race has evolved a great variety of methods of placing the entity in the way of making his own start. It has learned ways of lifting limitations sufficiently to permit effort; actual physical limitation. We have the way of surgery on a little skull pressure; of medicine in the stimulation of sluggish glands. Marvellous transformations of health and character are brought about by these means. But these are not free gifts, unless the impetus applied at the right spot can be so considered. There is no such thing as a free gift, even of opportunity. Our hypothetical entity is a mechanism which is on dead center. In him, says Gaelic, has come about "a state of equilibrium where, not the will but the power to apply pressure is lacking. The contribution (*i.e.*, the group contribution) consists merely in so placing the person that there is a chance of disturbing this equilibrium to permit once more individual application, no matter how small in outward seeming, as one touches the pendulum of a wound clock to start its machinery."

4.

All these considerations and principles that we have followed out in the compact microcosm of the family group apply exactly to wider inclusions. A man does not belong to one, but to many groups, attracted by affinity for the same reason that he belonged to his family—that the problem which is the cause of the group is one on which he can help.

"He is not merely one of a family," Gaelic expresses this, "he is a member also of a succession of ever more inclusive groups, until he is to be considered finally, as far as your earth life is concerned, a member of that which comprises the sum-total of earthly incarnations. Each of these groups has its own type of problems, good and evil, to be worked out, all of which have the same characteristics—that they are beyond the scope and power of individual solution, but may eventually be worked out by individual contribution toward solution. They have also the characteristic in common that they are the individual problem and responsibility.

"The exact form in which, and the exact manner in which they are proposed, are dependent upon the individual circumstance. The human being is born upon your planet and conditioned by its limitations because his state of being fits those limitations. He is born a Chinaman or an Arabian or an African or a Caucasian, and conditioned by the peculiar limitations which inhere racially, because his state of being fits more or less accurately those limitations. He is born into a family and is conditioned by the heredities of physical make-up, because his state of being finds a comfortable fit within those limitations. He is born with certain physical qualities of body which limit him in his possibilities, because his state of being does not, at that state of development, press beyond the bounds thus set for him."

In any of those larger groups, just as in the family, he must pass in review his evolutionary history. He must grow up, from the child to the youth, from the youth to maturity. In his youth we find him provincial, ignorantly arrogant toward what he lumps together as "foreigners," ineptly patriotic without thought that patriotism means aught but self-assertion, and blandly indifferent to the peoples beyond his border.

"Only a little broader is the Caucasian provincial within his race, is the Arabian proud and self-centered beneath his desert stars, is the African convinced that—whatever powers of magic the white man possesses—he alone is the great man of earth. And so the Chinaman, secure within his ages-old Oriental serenity, looks with contempt upon the 'foreign devil.' And so the human race in its youth bends its eyes downward toward its speck of earth and cries out against the few who raise their eyes."

In other words, humanity is still adolescent. To it we should accord the same tolerance we give the child in its family. We recognize its immaturity.

But as when the child grows into manhood, we are beginning to hope for a little more discrimination. "Man should by now be able to appraise and utilize what has up to now been unthinkingly a part of himself. And if he is able, by even ever so little, to work out a portion or a phase of group impetus, he has not only removed just so much limitation from the world, but he has also lightened the burden for his successors on this particular job and, naturally, qualified for a wider field himself."

CHAPTER V.

Conflict and Resistance

1.

SINCE WE are to work in groups—of greater or less inclusions, from family to race, as Gaelic says—how about the inevitable conflict of interests? How are they to be handled? Are we to be thorough-going pacifists and perpetually turn the other cheek? Or are we to resist aggression? Or are we even to become aggressors in order to reclaim our own?

Well, Gaelic pointed out first of all, resistance of some sort is necessary for development. We do not just work; we must have something to work on. The resistance need not be inimical. It may even be helpful. An airplane cannot rise without the resistance of the air.

The simplest example is what we have named ."the struggle for existence" in the biological setup. In nature, in order for one created thing to go on living another must die. "The condition of the hawk's existence involves the gathering of the shrew on which he feeds," says Gaelic. That is the hawk's business, to gather the conditions essential to its survival. One of the conditions is something to eat, and since a hawk is a carnivore that something has to be killed. But in essence the hawk is doing no different from any other creature in any other situation. In higher development conditions of mere survival are only part of life's necessity. There are also those conditions necessary to the fullest expression of inner nature. By inner nature Gaelic

said he means the quality of its consciousness—the individual
nature of itself that has been established in the course of its
race development. That development—of its quality of consciousness—has been earned through its own slow functioning
in evolution. For its further functioning, as well as for its continuing development, it has a variety of needs. The satisfaction
of these needs is legitimate.

"We will say that each entity occupies its own radius of life;
that which by its acquisition in evolution—or the acquisition
of its quality—it has so to speak *earned*. We are not yet touch-
ing that point of free will where right and wrong choice, from
the moral point of view, begins. But by the health of its effort,
the vigor of its quality, the perfection of its correspondences to
what it represents, its quality has nevertheless *earned* its place
in evolution. Now that place has a definite circle within which
it works. Any expression of itself within that circumscription is
in harmony, not only with its own being, but also with the
greater harmony of which it is a part. Conditions it finds within
that circle are its own to use, whatever they may be; for its
moral and legitimate use."

This is a reasonable proposition as long as we look at it
from only the point of view of the single entity. So considered
we see that the hawk's need for a shrew—or similar—is clearly
within its circle of existence. So it is entitled to the shrew. But
are we therefore to conclude that shrews are created for the
sole purpose of feeding hawks? Has not the shrew also a circle
of its own legitimate existence which its quality of consciousness has earned?

Here, Gaelic agreed, is where we "step out of the simple and
uncorrelated into an interplay in which the very gathering of
conditions fulfilling the intention of one thing at once modifies
some of the conditions fulfilling the intention of another thing."
Or stops them entirely, as in the case of our shrew! In other
words, there is an overlapping of these "definite and legitimate

circles." Gaelic did not dodge the issue. "Then," said he, "you get a spectacle of an apparent struggle or conflict in which many entities strive one against the other, each grasping with all its might for those things it needs, taking them when it can, wherever it finds them, irrespective of what other entities' interest in the matter might be."

Clear enough, we agreed; but where does common ordinary justice come in? Is this a case of sheer strength and brute force?

The apparent conflict, replied Gaelic in repetition of the figure, occurs because of the overlapping of the circles. The decision as to which will prevail does not depend on the entity's desire or even on his own unaided strength. It is a question of pressure at the point of conflict—the pressure of the all-inclusive Intention of the whole. If the harmony of the whole is balanced by the success of one, the other will lose. It is a question of contribution to the greater harmony. At this moment one does contribute, the other does not. "That," he added, "makes a picture of the *reason* for the struggle for existence in non-thinking nature."

We are not yet talking of human conflict, remember. We objected that the defeated creatures did not seem to get much out of it. How about them?

"That," said Gaelic, "is a fair question. How about those entities which appear to lose out in the struggle for existence? Whose very lives, perhaps, are obliterated as part of the conditions of manifestation of the other which for the moment happens to survive the conflict? The sentimentalist wants to know about that; the pessimist thinks it proves the universe is built on a system of iron and unjust warfare; the negative philosopher uses it as argument against any ordered and beneficent system at all.

"Do not forget," said Gaelic in rebuttal of this last, "that *up to a certain point in development*, the individual importance

is entirely subordinate to the quality importance." Nature sacri-
fices millions of specimens for the benefit of the species. And
sometimes—for a while anyway—it seems that the job of one
species is to further another. As though the shrew were indeed
created merely to feed the hawk. More often such a function is
part of the job. Sort of a stepladder affair rather than a simple
stepping-up.

Sometimes—indeed most often, Gaelic implied—in putting
a law into operation, we have to do considerable preparatory
work. We cannot merely invoke it. We have to build it up
through a series of preliminary laws. The law we are to use
must have a pedigree. Before the final law that results in a tree
can act, there must have acted a whole succession, beginning
with simple electronic substance, on up through the formation
of orbital systems, by way of planetary evolution, to the production of soil and climate which will permit the embodiment of
the tree intention.

"Each step of the process has required the action of numberless phases of law," said Gaelic, "and for each of these phases
conditions had to gather. Now, as I said, the interplay of these
various things is sometimes in more or less antithesis. If the
laws which are to result in one thing act fully, the laws which
would result in another thing are hampered, hindered, or perhaps estopped.

"Which intention shall prevail," he repeated his former statement, "depends not on the entity's desire, or on his unaided
strength, but on the pressure, *at that point,* of the greater,
all-inclusive Intention.

"Remember that the species is the important thing, the specimen the unimportant. We must postulate a two-fold process
in development. It is a good deal like a gas engine. We have
the compression stroke by which power is generated and the
expansion stroke by which the power is manifested. First one;
then the other. The same quality of consciousness (species)

whose one individual, caught in the compression cycle, suffered 'defeat' and extinction, will, in the expansion cycle when the time is ripe, be able to manifest itself in another and successful individual. In other words—to consider only two qualities, for the sake of simplicity—the quality that overcame in the first place may in its turn suffer defeat, and in that defeat supply to the other its conditions for manifestation.

"Of course," Gaelic pointed out, "the case is infinitely more complex, actually; but there is a rhythm of give and take, of pressure and expansion, of tempering and of full use throughout all created things. And remember that it is the Quality, not the individual creature, that so acts and reacts, and the individual case is of no final importance."

Remember, he is still discussing conflict in the natural world.

2.

That is the mechanism of what we call the struggle for existence as it operates in the material world. As far as mechanism is concerned, Gaelic assured us, man is in no different situation. That is to say, he "gathers within the radius of his life the conditions necessary to him for his complete manifestation, just as did the lower entities; and what he needs within his circle is his legitimately for the taking. Other circles overlap and sometimes overlay his own, and conflict results because of this. *In mechanism* there is no difference."

But actually there is a fundamental distinction. Man is not merely an interchangeable specimen of his kind. In case of robins, for instance, any robin anywhere in the world could be substituted for any other robin anywhere in the world, and it would not make the slightest difference. But men are not so standardized, nor indeed are some of the higher animals. They are persons rather than merely individuals. They possess a more perfected power of selecting. They can choose more freely; and therefore have what Betty calls "the blessed privilege of blundering." It is indeed a privilege, for without it one would be like the bees and the ants, caught permanently in a system.

The power to choose, in other words, may be exercised rightly or wrongly, but it lures to exploration, which in turn leads to new territory in development. But it also tempts us to grasp for "conditions of existence" outside that compact circle of legitimate occupation which our development has earned us and wherein we shall prevail. Then we are likely to run into trouble, for that territory may well be within the circumference of another's circle. If so, we probably shall get our heads bumped; which will at least warn us to get back in our own territory. In the process of getting our heads bumped, there is going to be a row.

"When," Gaelic worded this idea, "a man reaches in ignorance beyond his own circle, he encounters blind struggle, in which he cannot succeed. The benefit of his failure is to teach him that fact; and the use of that struggle is, not to gain power, but to teach him practically what I have just propounded in theory. If, however, he goes beyond his circle knowingly, graspingly intent on power which is not his right, he commits what you call a sin; not so much against those who dwell outside—for they have the whole cosmos back of them—but against himself alone."

While we are still in this predatory stage of our development we do a lot of this raiding, with malice and forethought, and possibly with considerable vainglory over our enterprise and prowess. Only lately is the idea beginning to gain ground that it may not be so gallant and praiseworthy a feat of arms. But, until by experience we learn, defeat seems to be the only way we can learn.

"It is not a pretty sight," said Gaelic, "but it is working out according to the intention of the method. Free will must choose, that is its very essence; and to choose, it must know. Otherwise it but grasps blindly in the dark that which first touches its hand. And knowledge can come only by actual experience. You may be inclined to dispute that statement, but it is a fact; and you have yourselves stated the thing inside out when you have said that you could be told nothing of which you were not already aware. Experience can be gained only by action; and new action, exploratory action, can be directed to a certain extent by analogy and experience and wisdom, but in the end there is always a residue of pure experiment. It is this residue of pure experiment which leads man beyond his circle ignorantly into conflict which (when it encroaches) must result in his defeat and at the same time, by that increase of knowledge, expands the circle."

If injustice apparently prevails, if it is the other robber baron who proves the stronger, and manages to beat a man on his own home grounds, even then the latter does not lose in the long run. "The compression gives him power."

"But," queried someone at this point of the argument, "how about ambition? aspiration? Is not that an attempt to surpass the limitations of one's circle?"

"Yes," admitted Gaelic, "that is where the residue of experiment comes in." A man who ventures in ignorance of what exactly his powers are, at least learns something. And increase in knowledge results in ultimate enlargement of the circle. Gaelic was not advising him to settle down in cushy comfort among his certainties. You cannot get experience except by action. "I do not necessarily mean *physical* action," said Gaelic. "But you cannot learn by mere talking."

That is why the life of the free will, the life with the privilege of blundering, is always so exciting. The circle defining the field of action of the lower creatures is clearly drawn. We are not so sure of our own. Right in the center of our circle we

are certain enough of ourselves, but we are never quite certain
where our outside periphery runs. The only way to find out is
to try.

"It is not a clearly defined circle," Gaelic impresses this, "but
an area of vaguely defined boundaries, fading in definition as
it extends outward into the unknown. The area of complete
self-knowledge is a compact though expanding nucleus which,
as it spreads, pushes before it, so to speak, the ill-defined penumbra about it. This penumbra, to pursue the figure, has not
as its boundary a balanced arc, but an irregular line, sometimes
extending far out in promontories, sometimes sticking at one
undeveloped point or another in deep bays.

"The effect of growth is two-fold: one to extend the clearly
and completely understood nucleus within which dwells rigid
responsibility, and the other to push outward boldly in experimental exploration."

3.

So there would seem to be really three kinds of conflict; what
might be called legitimate, illegitimate, and exploratory—
which may turn out to be either.

Legitimate conflict we undertake if that inner nucleus of
our complete self-knowledge is invaded. That is our own proper
possession. It comprises those things nutrient to our growth,
which cannot rightfully be appropriated by another. Within it
there is nothing which an outsider can find genuinely suitable
to himself which is not equally suitable to ourselves, and so
of mutual benefit. It is our right and duty to defend here
against invasion. "Whatever conflict then takes place," says
Gaelic, "is a righteous conflict against illegitimate aggression.
Your avoidance of that conflict is as much a sin as would be
unwarranted aggression on your own part. It is your duty to
fight with all the weapons at your command, within that area.
You need not fear defeat provided you put forth your full effort

and provided you restrain the field of combat to that area," Gaelic strongly emphasized the last words. The area, he redefined, is that of our "complete and satisfactory self-knowledge, however small that may be. It is an area of rigid responsibility; and it is the only area where we are held to a responsibility that is rigid. If you permit illegitimate aggression therein, you will always be able to recognize it as illegitimate, and you will be permitting a disharmony which is fundamental."

The second type—illegitimate conflict—is just the reverse. If knowingly we trespass another's "nucleus of complete self-understanding" just because we think we want something therein, we are ourselves raiders, and we shall get our heads bumped. There may be seeming initial success, but in the long run it will turn out to be defeat.

The third type—that of exploratory conflict—comes about because we cannot always be sure just where the various boundaries are. Our search properly to extend our own field may cause us to blunder. And the only way to find out is to try. We cannot profitably live cooped up in a rigid concentration camp of safety. But it must be in innocence. We have, says Gaelic, the duty and the pleasurable instinct, or passion, toward expansion and growth. This cannot be done primarily by building the walls of this inner self-awareness stone by stone a wee bit farther out; it can only be done by bold and joyous excursion into our outer circumferences in experiment toward that which calls the honest thing that dwells at the center. When the "compression of the life properly fulfilled within the center" has resulted in the generation of enough power, it must have its expression in expansion. "It is a rhythmic process," says Gaelic, "an attempt to perform either without the complete complement of the other results always in disaster." The expansion takes us out into unknown territory. Something there may be ours—or it may belong to someone else—or again someone else may be occupying it with no more than squatter's rights. Our attempt to follow our feelings of affinity, so to speak, must inevitably bring the clash of conflict. We may be quite honest in purpose; but since this is the area "outside complete knowledge," we do not really know. We may blunder and lose; or we may be right and win, but never without profit if in full honesty we have used our full effort. We cannot, without atrophy, huddle inside the sharp definition within which we are certain we must resist or sacrifice, defend or subdue ourselves into cooperation.

"Outside of that sharp definition," says Gaelic, "a man must reach by the boldness of his spirit, by the questing of his aspiration, by the grasping of his instinct for the unknown; uncertain, whatever the justness of his intuition, whether in that field on which he treads his unaccustomed foot he will win new spoil of victory for that which is divinely his own, or meet with the defeat and thrusting back which is inevitable at times to one who would explore. In the one case is the great happiness of acting, surely and with knowledge, in harmony; and in the other is the happiness following a great adventure."

If we do run into conflict it may be merely "a result of the overlapping overlying the fields of life of others, so that both are grasping for the same conditions but for opposing purposes. Whether one or the other will prevail depends on the needs in accordance with the Harmony of the moment.

"It is evident that were the field of possible conflict* the area of complete knowledge of both entities conflict would not take place at all, for the knowledge would convey to both an intellectual appreciation of the needs of harmony, so that cooperation rather than conflict would ensue. Only when one or the other of the entities involved is working outside the center of complete knowledge is there a struggle. Or when both are so working. The struggle is always beneficial, either in the

* i.e. through the desire of entities for the same conditions but for opposing purposes.

direction of compression for power, or for manifestation through success—either systole or diastole. Only when an entity *knowingly* grasps for that which is not its own, is there harm and confusion and disharmony.

"That is the general principle. It is necessary, however, to define more accurately the word *knowingly*. It does not mean, necessarily, that in any given case a man should consciously, deliberately, with malice aforethought, so to speak, go on a plundering expedition. It is much more subtle than that. In estimating any man's ignorance in the sense of his innocent reachings, we must estimate what faculties of moral knowledge actually exist in him as a being in a certain state of development, and to what extent he has in this case used those faculties. An omission to employ fully those criteria—methods of intelligent estimation and standards of human interrelation which his experience *plus* his natural moral aptitude have given him— is as serious an indictment against his innocence as the actual commission of a planned piracy might be."

4.

Gaelic never stated or implied that we necessarily go out looking for a fight; merely that we should expect—and welcome— resistance.

Conflict is only one kind of resistance. Resistance is a necessary ingredient of progress. Functioning means movement. Movement is always effort to overcome. Sometimes resistance is, in a manner of speaking, only apparent. When we are driving fast in our car, for example, we seem to ourselves—as indeed we are—meeting a tremendous resistance of the air. But when we stop, that resistance ceases. So, says Gaelic, we must distinguish emotionally. We must sometimes welcome rather than resent.

"It is not," says Gaelic, "so much an opposition as an indication that you do move. Only when you cease onward progres-

sion do you become part of the static and inert through which
you have been passing; and so the apparent resistance ceases.
Since this is, and always must be, a concomitant of living, one
of the first and most useful lessons to learn is that resistance
and opposition are not the same. The attainment of this simple
mental attitude removes from the resistance the elements of
struggle and of personality so that, instead of resenting it as a
bafflement, one welcomes it as a sure indication that one is
alive and forwardly in motion.

"The strength of apparent resistance, in its variation from
time to time, is sometimes an actual measure of speed of progress; sometimes a purely subjective misapprehension of the
amount of energy you are actually putting forth; and sometimes
a mere impatience of egocentricity resenting opposition. In the
majority of cases, whatever the external circumstances, the
sense of struggle as being stronger at one time than another, is
an illusion born of the greater or lesser degree of spiritual
integrity in command at that moment. When one feels borne
with a triumphant current, it is merely that one has entered
into, for the moment and fully, the realization of the nature
of resistance, and so rejoices in it, as the skilled player rejoices
in the difficulty of the game of his election. When, on the other
hand, he feels lost in the rack and battle and ill-fortune of over-
whelmment, it is because for the moment he has lost, in extraneous detail, his perception of the truth.

"One of the great simplicities which your world must teach
is the unimportance to the compactness of spiritual integrity
of any details. So that one realizes that no possible deprivation
or destruction of circumstance can deprive one of his place in
cosmos. For even beyond the ultimate deprivation of life itself remains still such of spiritual integrity as he has acquired;
and in due and fitting place.

"That successive deprivations of untoward chance, as it

seems to you, may be disagreeable and discomfortable, is readily to be admitted. That avoidance is sometimes desirable and worthy of man's best forethought and skill is indubitable. But fundamental harm can come from these things only if they move the spiritual integrity from its grasp on its simplicities."

CHAPTER VI.

The Spectrum of Consciousness

1.

SUCH ROUGHLY speaking is, according to Gaelic, the Job and the conditions of the Job. Before giving us any techniques as to performance, it seemed necessary to examine our natural equipment. What tools have we?

Well, we have certain natural instincts. We have our reasoning intelligence. We have—more vaguely—what we call our "intuitions."

Instinct could be succinctly defined as our racial memory of racial experiments and experiences. In the earlier stages of evolution the necessary experiments were performed wholesale, by the species, rather than as now by the individual. Millions of individuals tried, and failed, but each failure—stored and remembered in race-memory of their species—added to their race-wisdom. Myriads of bees did the wrong thing and perished, but in their destruction enriched their consciousness-degree—from which the succeeding bees were born and equipped—with new ideas as to the effective conduct of bees. Utilizing that stored wisdom the later bees meet the situation and do not die. They, as individuals, do not figure out the method. They do not learn it, as a child learns. They already *know*. They are, we say, possessed of *instincts*.

We humans also possess a certain body of instincts, developed in exactly the same manner, and utilized in exactly the same way. We do not learn them; we already know.

"Every day," reminded Gaelic, "the merest child is recollecting for its immediate purposes small fragments or bits of many millions of lives through which its human quality has passed. In the short space of two or three years, starting apparently with nothing at all, the human child acquires an immense store of knowledge. That knowledge is so habitual a portion of everyday living that you cease to wonder at it, and your evaluation of it is dulled. Nevertheless if you would for one day examine with a detached eye the detailed activities of a child, you could not but be struck by amazement at merely its muscular correlations and the ease and intelligence with which it performs feats of the body and mind which, were you to analyze them to their elements, would present a marvellously complicated accumulation of mere knowledge. The child, as you say, 'learns quickly'—so quickly that you are amazed at the facility. And were you to review the ordinary equipment for the simplest life necessary to any youth of twenty, you would sit down discouraged at the thought that in so few years so much must be inculcated. And you would have reason to be discouraged, were it not for the fact that from many incarnations—not necessarily personal to this one individual, but from many contributing incarnations of quality—experience and memory have been stored away for the use of recollection.

"If you are curious-minded enough, and philosophically enough inclined, you may trace introspectively what you have learned by in some manner having been a tree or a bird or a blade of grass or a living rock or whatever. And when in your daily life you employ any of these what you call primitive instincts, you are actually to that extent re-collecting a definite memory of a former incarnation of one sort or another."

Reincarnation in this sense, be it noted, not of yourself but of your species, of your kind. "Remember," warned Gaelic, "we deal with Quality, Intention, rather than individual persons."

However, for illustrations we need go no further than the physical mechanisms and functions. Our bodily instincts carry on bodily life with precision and accuracy. We do not have to study how to make our hearts beat; nor need we take thought on how our digestion is to function. The framework of successful life in such things is as reliably established for us as is the body politic of bees and ants.

But there is this difference: the bees and ants live wholly within that framework; we do not. Their body politic has, says Gaelic, "a perfection which enlists your admiration and is your despair. Man has not reached the political integrity of a column of ants, for they act entirely on instinct and instinctive actions are, almost always, surely and accurately wise in adaptation to the need. Consequently the lower forms of life fulfill that life with a beautiful precision which higher forms increasingly lack. This is not because of a degeneration from even proportionate wisdom on the part of the higher animal. It is because, as consciousness rises in evolution, the field of the precise instinctive action is narrowed, and the field of the reasoned—and blundering—experimental action is widened."

The lower forms of life have almost ceased experimenting. In experiment resides the possibility of blunder. As also of advance. The insect lives in his instinctive correspondences to life. "In man the instincts are reduced to the bare minimum necessary for self-preservation, and to him is accorded the privilege and the duty of experiment—and blunder. The things that are ready-made for him are his body and his bodily instincts. Both, from one point of view, are marvellous. From another, they are often clumsy. The rest is largely his.

"In the further development of consciousness," he predicted, "he will find his ready-made portion still more limited. He will make his own body, so to speak."

Gaelic checked himself at this point, but could not refrain

from adding one of what he called his "fructifying glimpses."

"I would add a great deal more, but I am warned I must not," said he, "I must say this very briefly—and too briefly. Just as the blundering but fairly successful experiments are synthesized, so to speak, into a gratuitous equipment of a higher order of beings, so does the process continue beyond yourselves. Your own original experiments or adaptations—as far as they are even successful to the degree of meeting conditions—enter the higher consciousness to be reverberated back toward the equipment of something beyond your ken."

2.

So the instincts are part of our equipment. Another, we led ourselves to believe, is what we call the mind. But Gaelic would not permit the distinction. If you are going to examine aspects of the mind, he suggested, it is only logical that you begin at the beginning and define what you are discussing. What is the mind?

"Consciousness (self-consciousness was his meaning here, I think) is an entity's awareness. Awareness requires a mechanism; just as any function requires a mechanism. Now how does anything become aware? It becomes aware by physical sensation, or response; by instinctive response; by intellectual response; by intuitive response; and by inspirational response— these divisions being purely arbitrary for the purposes of discussion," he hastened to add.

"Consider what you call white light. Broken up by a prism into the spectrum it shows as a series of separate colors, to which you give separate names, from the red at one end to the violet at the other, separating them arbitrarily into the different hues. Nevertheless, it is a fact that the spectrum presents an orderly progression of vibrations, without defined boundaries between any group of constituents, from one end to the other. The whole, taken together, undivided by the prism, you call one thing—white light."

For discussion Gaelic postulated our bit of all-consciousness —the white light within us of divinity—refracted by our individuality into its components, just as physical white light is split by the prism.

"So your consciousness," he continued, "which is in manifestation your awareness, progresses in orderly unbroken fashion from the red of physical sensation to the ultraviolet of the highest aspiration. And if you are functioning through the nerves and contacts of your physical body, your awareness-response is through sensation. If you are functioning in a different portion of the spectrum *the same response in kind*, you receive through the blue or green of what you call intellect. And if your awareness-response is received through those higher powers of which you are but primitively gaining control, you are receiving the same response in kind through intuitive faculties or through what you call direct inspiration.

"Thus from one end of the scale to the other you are simply traversing one and the same thing—what we call the white light of consciousness. This white light of consciousness is refracted through the physical manifestation of quality. Without this manifestation you have the Inunderstandable, the white light of Cosmic Unity, which you have variously named as All-Consciousness, All-Spirit, or God. In this aspect you may call it the All-Wisdom, the All-Intelligence, the All-Perception of All-Possibility. Refracted through the physical manifestation of quality, it becomes a spectrum in which the entity dwells; and at various points in which the entity centers its individuality according to its state of development—and in a very limited way according to its choice.

"We may conceive the simplest creature, or bit of consciousness, starting at the dullest red and progressing slowly, slowly in the course of its evolution along its rainbow path through the various phases of awareness-responses. And you must remember that, like the spectrum, there are no dividing lines. There are no dividing lines between the senses and the mind and the intuition and the inspiration. And it does not matter how you subdivide the mind into what you call the subliminal, the superliminal, the superconscious, the subconscious or whatever; or the physical responses into this, that or the other hair-splitting categories of your physiologists. It matters not. They blend one into the other in orderly progression; and the reason one appears as red, or sensation, and another as blue, or mind, and another as violet, or inspiration, is not because of a differentiation in the thing itself, but because of the constitution of the perception-mechanism which happens to be more or less predominant in the particular manifestation of the entity from whose point of view it is examined.

"In this analysis we have, for greater clarity, merely considered the *human* mind," Gaelic pointed out, "rather than Mind itself. From the human point of view," said he, "we have arranged our spectrum to comprise the awareness-mechanics of Sensation, of Instinct, of Intellect, of Intuition, and of Inspiration. Of these, the 'red' end, or sensation, might from one point of view be defined as almost a mechanical and automatic response to stimuli. The rock, subjected to certain influences, of heat, cold, or moisture, responds invariably in a certain manner. Progressing to the next higher step, we see in exactly the same manner, the most primitive organisms responding automatically and invariably to given stimuli. Surrounding an insect with certain conditions of sun-warmth, or of other climatic or material impactions, a predictable and uniform action may be expected. That is pure instinct.

"The birth of Intellect, as distinguished from this type of automatic response, coincides with the first appearance of free will. Free will is that mechanism by which an organism of advancing complexity is enabled to segregate and select, from the superabundance of responses made possible by that complexity, in the direction of its most insistent need and development. A complex mechanism—to repeat this thought in other words—has within itself points of possible contact in a multitude of directions beyond the simple needs of its mere animal or vital requirements. And beyond its capacity of assimilation, were all to be accorded equal attention and response. The faculty of intellect is the selecting instrument among these superabundant multiplicities. And, naturally, it functions through what you have named as free will. Have I made myself clear?

"Very well. The exact point in our figurative spectrum at which any consciousness possessed of free-will, in however small a degree, is for that period centered, is that consciousness' *point of intellect*.

"The point *above* that center of consciousness is the point of the supraconscious mind of that entity; related to its conscious intellect in exactly the same way that *your* supraconscious mind is related to your own conscious mind. And as the center of consciousness, which is the center from which that individual entity makes its selections, moves on up the scale of vibrations, which constitutes the spectrum, it enters the field of what *has* heretofore been, its supraconscious, and renders that erstwhile supraconscious into its selecting conscious.

"This being the case, you can readily deduce a wider significance in our statement of last year, when you learned that your supraconscious is to *our*selves (Invisibles) what the conscious is to *you* in your physical body. That did not mean that in entering *our* estate, your supraconscious mind in its present aspect of relationship to yourselves would then become your predominating intellectual instrument. It merely meant that those powers and relationships and cosmic contacts which now exist in your intuitional region, so to speak, will be transferred into an intellectuality which will possess the same selecting and applying powers of individual free-will which you now recognize and employ in your conscious mind of today. And above that center still will be another appreciable, but only partly translatable, field of awareness which perhaps you may call 'intuitional.'

"The conscious mind, then," Gaelic summed up his distinction, "is the focussing point in that environment which at the moment supplies the need of the entity. The Intellect—the conscious mind of yourselves—is that which focusses sharply on the physical. Outside of that the Mind—*the same Mind*—is blurred, so to speak."

As a corollary, that focus may be shifted, altered. Normally this is done in due course of development. It is moved along the spectrum.

"Our conscious mind," Gaelic referred to his own "discarnate" state of existence, "is that which focusses on *our* state of consciousness, or environment."

In certain cases this shift of focus may be temporarily accomplished, we were led to suppose, by "occult" knowledge.

"We," said Gaelic, "are able to move that focus, more or less. Some of you a little."

This analysis we found very exciting. Indeed, one of our members paced up and down beating his head in vexation.

"It's so simple, so clear, so reasonable!" he cried. "Why couldn't I think of it myself!"

CHAPTER VII.

Gaelic's Four Rules

1.

OUR PIOUS forefathers stoutly maintained that our afflictions are due largely to a "state of sin" which results from an earlier "fall from grace" on the part of still more distant forefathers. As a matter of fact, states Gaelic, discomfort of any kind is usually an incentive to get busy and remedy things; and hence a desirable spur to growth. It is also sometimes a pretty good symptom that we are busy, that we are experimenting, exploring, pushing ahead. Discomfort, pain, unhappiness are not per se helpful to growth; but they may well be a mark of growing.

Evolution is largely a matter of adaptation, of trying out expedences. No creature, or entity, or force, or quality of consciousness, said Gaelic, starts right from the beginning, on its own, to evolve an apparatus to fit its needs. It uses as foundation and as material the simple experiments along the same lines of the simpler qualities of consciousness that have preceded it. To their successes it adds its own contribution. That is the course of evolution from the simple to the more complex, by means of groping partially successful experiment based on more nearly perfected experiments of the past, which in their day also blundered.

Even successful result of experiment is at first rough. Use smooths it out. The whole process is repetitive. Millions of individual small successes became at last part of the race-wisdom of the ant, in which all ants can function. That ant race-wisdom is available to all finite creation. It becomes part of the Idea of the whole body of finite consciousness, material for use in experiment by higher creatures than the ant. And so on up.

And like the ant since we are *becoming*, and experimenting, we fail a hundred times in order to succeed once. Most experiments are unsuccessful, or only partially successful. The corollary is always discomfort. Discomfort varies in degree, from mere uneasiness to actual suffering. When any creature is uncomfortable, it tries to do something about it.

But discomfort, pain, unhappiness are more than a spur to effort. They indicate incompleteness, like ugliness in art. Their resolving will lie in the direction of harmonious larger inclusions. When the experiment is finally successful, they will disappear.

So the first universal blind urge to progress is based on simple self-interest. Only with the broadening of intelligence, the expansion of wisdom, do we perceive that it subserves a greater purpose than the ease of comfort. To repeat the concept, when an Idea has been conceived, adequately embodied, repeated enough so that its mold is solid and assured, it becomes a contribution. A fully completed experiment becomes eventually an *instinct,* a property of race-wisdom, at the service of the whole scheme. On its solid foundation may be built another venture, toward a higher construction.

In this manner we understand discomfort as the first of the aids to our Job, an incentive to effort.

2.

Our escape from the discomfort of incompletion, then, depends on our becoming and remaining active, which ties in with all of Gaelic's previous talks on the importance of functioning. He desired now to add certain small suggestions to ease the effort.

In the first place, the very idea of "effort" is a bad one. You can do things under strain, says Gaelic, but they are rarely effective or permanent. Indeed, he added, "the limitation implied by the feeling of strain is one imposed in order to confine effort within the effective!"

Strain is a danger signal that we are beginning to be futile. "It is likewise," said Gaelic, "a warning that one is stepping outside the task of which he is capable at the moment. Work done under strain is never work permanently completed, but is at best in the nature of a scaffolding." If it seems to you possible to accomplish only "by getting exhausted, it indicates," said Gaelic in his stately fashion, "that your vision has embraced too large a segment of your task." Or, more colloquially, we have bitten off more than we can chew. "It is well then," continues Gaelic, "to retrace in aspiration to within the bounds of the comfortably attainable. Accomplishment beyond the comfortably attainable"—he considered the point important enough to repeat—"is an illusion, for it results in nothing of solid permanence. It is well to wait, within the permitted territory, the growth in power until one feels able to advance with sure and easy steps. If there seems pressure to exceed comfortable accomplishment, then be certain the pressure comes, not from aspiration, but unbalance."

So the first rule is: *Work within your powers.*

3.

Things do not, should not, proceed uninterruptedly. They move in rhythm, always. That is the method of functioning—go—stop, go—stop, like the heartbeat. It traces back to Betty's fundamental of Frequency. And as each created thing has its individual frequency, "so different types of effort have their own rhythms. The trick is to catch them at their peak and relinquish them wholly at their natural ebb. Any attempt to fill that ebb by effort in order to induce a smooth continuous level of accomplishment results merely in checking the forward free natural

movement of the waves. That is a very ornamental way of saying you get 'stale.' "

Refreshment. All work and no play—the old proverb. And
the materials of refreshment are always close at hand in the
simple things about us. To them we lift our eyes when we look
up from our work, and we should take them for what they are
meant to be, without analysis, for their enjoyment alone. Betty
best expressed this, and I quote here from one of the records
of her own work.

"You know a child's first impulse, when you give it a beautiful flower, is to pull it to pieces," said an Invisible, through
her. "That is natural enough, but a flower is not to be handled
that way: it is to be enjoyed whole, as an inspirational thing.
These foreshadowed ideas that come are delicate things, blossoming things. They must have more effect on the inspirational
side and less in concentration of pulling them to pieces to
understand. The constant emphasis is *always* in putting most
attention and energy on the *influence* of the idea: how to absorb it and assimilate it and take it to yourselves. That is the
important work on each one; and the dissecting of it is only
allowable after the rainbow influence, or the flower influence,
has entered into you.

"So many beautiful things are put into the world solely to
help you take the jump-off. I took the rainbow because it seems
so obviously inaccessible that no one could dream of spoiling it
by reaching and analyzing it. It was balancing in visioning. It
is the refreshments of life that you should take joyously and
vitally. The beauties of things teach you how to liberate your
spirit. You ask how you can feel free and happy. Can you
not relive the moments you responded most keenly to beauty?
Doesn't that give you some idea of the technique of springing
off beyond yourself? There is your guide to the way. And
strangely enough it is a circular thing; because, having sprung
loose in response to inspiration or beauty, the refreshment and

replenishment of it arouses the spark of vitality, which—in its turn—through its entirely practical methods—will help you to climb with understanding and desire, not baffled and strained and drawn. You have oxygenized and energized, have made a natural process of what was a puzzle and a tangle and an effort. You must not starve that rainbow side. It is more practical than you think. It is the mechanism of liberation."

"I am refreshing myself," said Betty. "They are showing me how to refresh myself in a confined place, such as a prison cell. Still it is possible to have rainbow feelings there. There are pieces of color around, separate soft colors, and it gives me a different sensation when I dive—delve—into them.—A fern; just a long green fern with little tender clinging tips that speak of growth in a perfectly suitable environment. That is one. There are so many things. I can't stop to tell you how playing with them liberates you. There is Nimrod (the cat). He is good for that, too: even his whiskers are amusing."

"You must not deny your rainbow soul its playtime," resumed the Invisible. "If you only realized what wings grew during its playtimes; and how glad you are to have them, even when you have to fold them for practical work."

"I'd always like to have a sheath," observed Betty, "—I suppose they're clothes—of satisfying texture around me."

"Yes," agreed the Invisible, "clothes for the sake of enlivening your spirit and not for the eyes of fashion. It all helps. Don't scorn little things: indulge them. If you have a secret tiniest leaning toward what seems a madly inappropriate idea, try indulging it for the sake of liberating your impulses.

"Nothing is right if your proportion is not right. There is something so simple I want to say to you. It is on the question of one simple thing to do when you are puzzled or baffled or congested. And that is this: look up from your work. When everything else around you may tangle up or bother, you can still know your ultimate intent; you can look at the end of the

road. You can always concentrate on your intent, your vista
That is one of the rules.

"That intent is a big thing. It keeps us individually from
prisoning ourselves in all those painful convolutions in the same
place. Looking up, and forward, with intent, never mind how
baffled you may be. It is our collective intent with this group
that will accomplish."

So Gaelic formulated his second rule: *look up from your
work.*

4.

Look up from your work from time to time if only for a moment. When we learn how to do that properly, we shall begin
to catch the principle of that rhythm which is so integral a part
of successful activity. But the actual process is more complicated than just catching the cadence of one great master beat.
There is the big wave, to be sure; but, says Gaelic, "all the big
waves have loads of little waves on their surface and each of
these little waves has its rhythm. We will take a present example to make that clear. You realize perfectly that every one
of its days has its rhythm, and you more or less accommodate
yourself to that. You are working with us now but you would
not try to work with us all day. You catch the peak for an hour
and then you do something else in the way both of work and
of recreation. That, as you say, distracts you and freshens you
so that tomorrow morning you are ready for another go at it.
Now the thing I want to point out is that, just as this little wave
of possible accomplishment exists in the day, so it is a part of
a larger wave of accomplishment which must have its peak and
ebb. It may seem logical that if, by a balanced refreshment, you
keep yourself from too great effort in any one day and arrive
at the next day thoroughly refreshed, you should be able to go
on with an indefinite series of such days. That is not true. The
larger rhythm must also be allowed its swing.

"The point is, when you get your rhythm you will arrange so that you don't controvert it any more than you have to. You work toward it all the time.

"Now this is difficult. These rhythms are not quite in your time element. By the very nature of rhythm they must have symmetrical regularity—pulsation—but that regularity is not made up of time, it is made up of pressure and release. Let's put it baldly: one wave of effort might last three weeks with you and the next one last two days, yet they would be equal in themselves. It is partly fourth dimensional. It is not exactly intensity, it is the quality of the thing. The nearest I can come to it is that, in diagramming your rhythm, you would have to transpose the quality of the thing accomplished into the terms of space in the diagram, and hence of time, of course. I fear this is not transferable except in a glimpse," Gaelic admitted.

Nor, it seemed, do we actually go at it as a diagrammatic problem. It is here stated as such merely for general understanding. In the actual catching of rhythm we do not figure it out any more than a good dancer mentally fits his steps to the sway of the music. "The intellect has not even a look-in!" stated the Invisibles with great emphasis. "This is final!" We develop, or acquire—or perhaps are endowed with—a feeling for rhythm. Especially we develop it. "You have to depend *entirely* on the judgments suggested to you by your feeling, if you have a feeling for rhythm. You will work harmoniously, provided you listen to the rhythm. If not you are out of luck, for the moment. The artist plans the rhythm of his work unconsciously, by feeling. He feels about how much he has in him, and the proportions of what he is doing seem somehow to arrange themselves so that they pretty closely coincide with his feeling of the ebb of creative energy, which means a forcing if he goes beyond it. He hits it more or less according to his subtle and instinctive inunderstood sense of rhythm, great and small.

"Your own problem is to adapt, as perfectly as possible, the job to the rhythm. If it cannot be comprised within the dynamics of one upsurge, then it must be planned to be accomplished in a series of efforts, and must be imbued with a rhythm of its own of such nature that its natural breaking-off points, so to speak, will coincide with your own natural ebb. A badly conceived effort does not sink naturally at the time of that ebb, and requires forced efforts beyond the limits of your own rhythm. If it is badly planned and you drop it, you have a jagged edge."

Sounds a good deal, he confessed, like that centipede in the old jingle who began to think of which leg moved first, and ended in the ditch.

"But remember," he offered as encouragement, "that this sense of rhythm is an accompanying product of the increasing consciousness of and knowledge of and living in general harmony. It is nothing else; and it comes in no other way. As to its acquisition, therefore, we can say no more than that we are striving constantly with you to lead you into it.

"This attempted glimpse today is not to set you a puzzle for your mind's manipulation, but to reveal to you an aim, cloudy, misted and undefined though it may be, toward which to turn your farther aspirations. And perhaps to afford you an encouragement on the way."

By way of further encouragement some Invisible spoke the following beautiful piece.

"Vibrations are life, and waves are progress in life. The thing that is made by vibrations moves within the limits of its being, and also carries forward—through itself and its contacts —the wave.

"Waves lift and fall, as well as move forward; and the particles that comprise them are also elevated and depressed, as well as carrying through themselves the forward movement.

The rise and fall is in itself rhythmic and harmonious. Without it no forward movement is possible. This is a universal law, applying to the mighty and on-sweeping tide of cosmic evolution, and alike to the little ripples in the tiny pools that make up individual affairs. The sea gull that exults upward on the shoulder of the rising wave, too often, instead of falling in glory of grandeur into the trough, plunges from its height darkened with despair—because it has not the vision to see, nor the perception to feel, the mighty, slow-gathering force that will lift it again to another moment of high-tossing, sun-glinted height.

"This is a universal law.

"Know that. Understand that. Accept the recession into the quiet hollows, into the slow-sucking trough, as part of the great rhythm, without which there would be stagnation. Learn to take it as the repose period, the gathering period, the period in which the mighty forces that lift the wave upward, are quietly, powerfully coming in. If you could only once feel this, visualize it, never again could you be uneasy, depressed, low spirited, discouraged, merely because of the natural, inevitable, necessary ebb after the flow. Never again would you worry because in this or that your powers of today are not your powers of yesterday, that your wings are folded, that a darkness seems to have closed you about. Accept the quietude, accept the ebb —enjoy it, as all harmonious things should be enjoyed. Rest in confidence with your folded wings, knowing that it is the law; that soon beneath your breast the stir of gathering forces must be felt; sure that in the progress that the law ordains you *must* once more be swept upward by the glittering crest, whence all horizons are far, and the whistling winds of eternity tempt again your outspread wings.

"As I said, this is the universal law. By it you can measure your smallest moods. By it you can measure your greatest griefs and despairs. Carry it always with you, for its fitting is to all occasion."

So here we have the third rule: *we must work in rhythm.*

5.

Originality in effort is all very well, says Gaelic; indeed it is the very essence of progress. But that does not mean we should feel called upon to do everything fresh from the beginning. We would not dream of so asinine a procedure as forging our own nails if we were building a fence; we would go to the hardware store and buy some. In the same manner we may gain much by following grooves already worn for us, instead of insisting on cutting new ones. Nor is there sense in doing things differently merely to be different. Latterly, in revolt against regimentation, we have been inclined to do just that, to shy off violently from the word *ritual.*

But, objected Gaelic, ritual is merely a common denominator of cooperation. In work too great for one man's handling he must find help from others, and sometimes he is most effective within the ritual to which these others have subscribed. It makes things easier. And it is not necessary to make ritual sacrosanct. It may indeed rate that importance, but on the other hand it may be, as Gaelic expresses it, "merely an emollient of intercourse, unimportant in itself except for that purpose. That is the value of the human tendency toward uniformities even in the apparently trivial; such as the custom of the moment as respects clothing, manners, personal decoration and the point of view as to the commonplaces. Valuable as the quality of individuality is, it is absurd to waste its dynamics on the things that do not matter. It is worse than absurd to insist on it in those things when such insistence inhibits or deflects or calls attention unnecessarily among those whose forces would be better expended in cooperation.

"In this sense all outward forms and customs are ritual, and are never intrinsically either good or evil, to be fanatically adhered to, or as fanatically deprecated. Each age, each segment of consciousness has its own ritual, adopted by majority consent for the moment. It is effective when it fulfills its function of automatically smoothing the attritions of unimportance. It should never be combatted through motives of personal taste or aversion. It becomes of sufficient importance for that only when it ceases to fulfill the function just described. Individuality of soul is a mark of development: eccentricity of externals is only a mark of eccentricity. If you were to visit another planet, you might consider it absurd and beneath your dignity to paint your face sky blue, but a failure to do so might set you apart from those to whom you were accredited. Your failure to conform would be submerging your purpose in the trivial. One of the best weapons of deterrent forces is to inject into the human consciousness small windmills at which to tilt, tempting it to remain behind for that purpose instead of going on. The most effective windmills are those of outgrown ritual."

I do not know quite how to epitomize this last of Gaelic's small suggestions. Possibly *don't be a crank* would do.

CHAPTER VIII.

"The Archangel and the Bird"

1.

It will be remembered that Gaelic had considerable to say about false self-sacrifice. He had no use for it. As emphatically he had no use for making decisions for other people. Nor for asking other people to make decisions for us. That applies to our relations with the Invisibles as well as our fellow men here. The only reason we are on earth is to get a chance to grow, to develop, to "make character," as they say. The tool for development is the free will; and the use of free will is to make decisions. A lifetime affords room for just so many decisions. If we ask somebody else to make one of them for us we are deliberately throwing away one chance. If we permit someone to decide for us, we permit him to rob us as definitely as though he had dipped into our pocket.

"The matter of decisions is a matter of development, and even a mistaken decision may result in considerable advancement. You move by making your mistaken decisions or your happy choices, as the case may be," was the way Gaelic expressed this. "If by making a person's decision for him, of any kind, you have deprived that person of a certain opportunity and therefore a certain property, you have robbed him, with the best intentions in the world. He may thereby gain certain easements unearned, but at the same time he has been forced

95

to forego a chance for certain self-building which the process of earning would have accomplished for him."

But such mistaken zeal has even wider effect than the merely personal.

"Taken in the group sense," says Gaelic, "this thing you have presented him, this thing you have prevented him from doing, is in the group impetus still undone. It remains to be done, and must await another combination of circumstances making that thing possible. That may not recur until after a considerable time, and the group is burdened with the effects until that time has come. That is for the group aspect.

"Now as to the personal aspect: in the law of compensation sooner or later you must make restitution in kind for whatever you have appropriated. Sometime in your two histories an extra effort from yourself for the other will be demanded and must be made, when condition and opportunity serve. This apparently gratuitous service accounts for most of the responsibility for others outside of the natural affection and desire. It is the affinity which you will probably recognize.

"As to the assumption vicariously of the immediate consequence of that which you have arbitrarily taken from the other, that may well happen. But it will not be by way of any immediate compensatory balance. It is merely because unguarded you have stepped too close within their zone of action. You did not belong within that zone of action, remember, and unless your insulation is strong it probably will come about that you will be affected."

"How," asked someone, "does one know the difference between the service which you owe, and that for which you are going to owe later?"

"That is a very pertinent question," replied Gaelic. "The gratuitous service that one owes comes about in such a way, when the conditions are ripe, that one is forced to pay it by force of circumstance. You have the general principle of offer and appropriation for your ordinary guidance.

"It is both undesirable and unwise, and indeed unwarranted, to supply any man with a ready mechanical measure into which he can feed his problems and from which he can withdraw a ready-made decision. *Decision is the vital principle of individual progress, and cannot be taken out of the individual's hands without a far-reaching harm.*"

Naturally the withholding of this sort of specific advice on detail may often result in a much less effective course of action, externally. That is unimportant. The privilege of blundering, Gaelic reminded us again, is one of our most precious possessions. There may be apparent loss. But it must be remembered, said he, "that you may be deterred, or stopped; but what solid acquisition you have made is yours eternally. The strings of your lute may be tuned higher, but they can never be slacked."

"What then of deterioration through the neglect or misuse of capacity?" asked someone. "Might not that slack the string?"

"You deter. You stop," Gaelic assured him. "You proceed on the next step with infinitely increased difficulty. You do not lose. You can deteriorate your immediate potentiality, and the instruments by which that potentiality might be assured. The gain you make, you hold."

2.

Occasionally, to drive home a point, Gaelic would tell us a story, a sort of parable. He did this with considerable gusto and a quaint and solemn style and humor all his own. This matter of giving advice was one such occasion.

"This afternoon," he began, "I will make you a magic. I will tell you a tale. For the telling of a tale is the gathering of what never was into a thing that will endure. And if that be not magic, what is?

"It happened in the days of the first legend of all; when God made the heavens above, and the earth beneath, and all that in them is.

"And he called to him on his seventh day of rest the greatest of his archangels, who had stood at his right hand while he fashioned the wonders of his creation; and he said to that Archangel:

" 'Lo, here are my creatures, who live, but possess no knowledge of the destinies to which they are called. Thou hast stood at my right hand, and thou knowest that which I purpose. Go, thou and thy brethren, unto each and every creature, great and small, and to him impart that knowledge which thou hast of me, as to the means by which he shall fulfill his destiny.'

"And the archangels descended to the earth, undertaking this instruction. For lo, each creature existed according to his kind, numb, dumb and unaware. So this Archangel called to him one of the creatures of God's fashioning, and he said to him:

" 'Lo, here I am, by command, to teach thee that which thou must know in order to function thyself according to the purposes of God.'

"And they sat them down together.

"And first the Archangel taught concerning cunning things, showing how levers act, conveying power, through the angles of their mechanism. Thus ended the first week.

"And the Archangel took up the lengthening and shortening of muscular fibre, and the application of will to move them. And there ended the second week.

"And then he explained very carefully the opposition of forces, how one working against another at a given angle produces a third, extending between the two. And thus ended the third week.

"Next he brought forward the principles of gravitation, showing in process and beautiful mathematical formulae how particles attract each other and in what proportion to their masses. And there ended still another week.

"Nor was the instruction yet ended; for the principles of equilibrium were next, not touched upon, but followed to their final resting place among the inner arcana of physical science. And there ended even another week.

"And the creature with whom the Archangel thus labored studied these things, and knew them—because it was the will of God, and certainly for no other reason.

"Then the Archangel, having finished his task, said to the creature:

" 'The time has come: the knowledge of your structure and capabilities is now complete. Proceed to function.'

"And the creature looked upon the Archangel in puzzlement, knowing not what next to do.

"And God, resting from his labors, looked upon the creation he had made and found it still numb, and dumb and unaware. And he descended in the Spirit of Wisdom: and he asked: 'Lo, these many weeks have passed, and still no one of my creatures stirs toward his appointed destiny.'

"And the Archangel answered to him, 'Lo, I have given of all necessary knowledge; and still here sits this creature thou hast made, fixed to earth. I have urged him, but he will not fly.'

"And with that word a strange and wonderful thing happened, for up from the earth and into the air sprang the bird. Up into the air he circled, beating his wings. He swung down his long free arc; he turned short up against the breeze; with rapid wings he hovered at one place; and at the last, straight as an arrow up into the blue he shot until, a mere speck in the sky, he was almost lost to view. Long time he was gone, but at last, in wild free flight, straight back to earth he came, and with a rush of air through outspread pinions he dropped once more beside the Archangel. And the Archangel said to him:

" 'But why, when you had learned, did you not obey?'

"And the bird said to him: 'I obeyed when you told me the purpose of God's intention.'

"And the Spirit of Wisdom descended into that bird, and he spoke to the Archangel with the voice of God. And the Archangel said:

" 'The things you have learned from me, you have learned well.'

"But the bird replied: 'The thing I learned of you, you knew not that you taught. And the Word I learned from you, you did not utter until the last. All the knowledge which has so delayed the beginning of God's purpose were to me forgotten things when I mounted toward the heavens.

" 'You need have told me but simple things, and of those simple things I must have been aware. It would have been enough to have made me know that I had wings, that the sky is above, and to have pointed to the sun.'

"Then said the Archangel: 'Our labor has been in vain.'

" 'Not so,' said the Spirit of Wisdom within the bird. 'It will be all very interesting to think about—when I am on the ground.' "

Those present agreed that this was a most entertaining magic.

"We are all birds," said Gaelic, "and we have within call the Archangels of Knowledge. From them we can never learn to fly. By ourselves we should never become aware, but should sit numb and dumb, as in the days of the old legend. From the Spirit of Wisdom we must learn only a few and simple things: the Purpose, the wings, and the air which shall sustain our flight. It will be very interesting to think about our 'stresses and strains and torsions,' our mathematical equations, the machinery of our functions—when we are sitting on the ground.

"Everything is mathematical—everything. Music is a harmonious arrangement of vibrations, according to mathematics. A skillful mathematical physicist should be able to write perfectly harmonious music in the form of equations, grouping his vibrations, which represent tones, according to those equations. And when manifested in sound, it would be harmonious music. But it would not leave the ground. It is so with every other human contact with Reality. Mathematics can express only the vehicle of Intention, not Intention itself. As a method of intellectual understanding its point of view has great importance; but it is not the point from which to approach creative functioning in anything, whether flying, or music, or living one's life in accord with harmony. The creature must have knowledge of its equipment; it must have knowledge of its field and direction of endeavor. That is all. Then it must be told the Intention: 'Fly!' 'Sing!' 'Live!'

"And it does not matter one bit whether he ever knows the mathematics of it or not.

"Give people their faith, a knowledge of their constitution, and hence their equipment, as far as it is necessary to support that faith. Give them the direction of their effort; and toss them into the air! In the glory and joy of flight they will find the energy and the exultation of their effort.

"Is my parable both amusing and instructive?" enquired he.

"Both! Very!" cried all.

CHAPTER IX.

The Core of Harmony

1.

WHAT KIND of a job can we best work on? What sort of thing will best serve the constructive purpose? A great many conscientious people ask that question.

Anything, said Gaelic; anything at all that fits the individual equipment, he amended. There is nothing too trivial, too small to contain the possibility of full spiritual values. The thing itself is of no importance in the long view. It is what we do with it that is important. Someone objected that a child born in the slums is in handicap.

"The circumstances of birth have nothing to do with the matter," said Gaelic categorically. "That is a frequent mistake— the idea that a person is placed in harmonious or disharmonious circumstances for the sake of development." Circumstances are efficient for development "according as the pressure," said he. That is what counts—the pressure we use against the resistances by which we rise.

"The mere fact of even moderate cheerfulness," he exemplified, "in squalid circumstances is a force of development, sometimes, that is exceedingly strong; whereas cheerfulness in thoroughly pleasant and congenial surroundings has no developing power whatever. Why? Because it is working against no pressure.

"So do not mistake; for every circumstance there is compen-

103

sation. Take your slum influence on the young and innocent child. You see him little by little yielding to the evil about him, until you say, 'He is a lost soul.' Perhaps so. But if that is literally a fact, he would be a lost soul anywhere.

"If, however, step by step—even though forced back to the very wall—he has put forth the free will of resistance, the repercussion of that force has had its due effect; and, though materially and apparently spiritually he may end as a criminal, until the power of circumstance has been weighed against the power of resistance, and the ratio evaluated, you cannot judge."

2.

Gaelic was by no means arguing that the worse the circumstances, the better the job. That would be absurd. Merely that we can find our job, if we will, no matter what our circumstances, and that it *can* contain the full possibility of our growth and development; that when we manage to define it, and to work at it within our powers, without strain, we are fulfilling our obligation of functioning, and we are happy. Happiness is an inner thing. It is not an attitude of action toward externals. It is a state of being. And that state of being we call a condition of harmony.

"This state of being," said Gaelic, "may be best understood by considering some fragment of life divested of all but simplicities. Not that a state of harmony depends upon such a divestment, but merely to convey an understanding of the pure quality. Hark back within your experience, each within himself, to some time when, for a greater or lesser period, a month, a week, a day, even an hour, life has seemed so simplified as to flow forward without the necessity of impulse, and without the constrainment of taking thought; with no time appointments to meet, with no dutiful calls to answer, and yet not devoid of the activities natural and appropriate to that spiritual spaciousness. At such times has it not seemed to you, perhaps, that you experienced a certain overflow beyond the boundaries of your workaday tight personality, to include a concurrent progression, arm-linked in kinship, with those things about you that are pacing with you in like rhythm? So, whatever happens, you move toward and through with a certain satisfied inevitability? with no apprehension, and equally with no externalized appreciation? accepting their concurrence as you accept your indrawn breath? I am assuming a space of time at which the sharp-toothed demands of life have not gnawed."

Gaelic insisted on distinguishing this "simple pure state of being" from emotional ecstasy, or a sort of mentally acknowledged happiness, or any deliberate appreciation, esthetic or otherwise. "These may be," he acknowledged, "occasional offshoots or concomitants of the state of being." But they are not the thing itself.

"This you may perhaps recognize in its uttermost simplicity as the state of being which we call harmony. It is a flowing, not a static contentment. This is the underlying structure of a life attuned, in whatever degree, to harmony. Overlaid is the substance of life itself, with all its activities of mental responses. These mental responses are directed toward the practical problems of which the world is composed. These may be agreeable, in tune with your temperament; and so you find pleasure and —yes—happiness in their functioning. They may be antagonistic or annoyingly frustrating or even corroding; and so, in the incompletion, they make for clash and discord. They may be constructively directed, adding to the mold of creative fashioning; or they may be destructive, even down to that darkness wherein man grips his enemy fast and finds it is his own soul. But all these things have not to do with harmony or disharmony, unless you elect to make them so. For the reason, that the mechanism of them is in the consciously directed mind; and the state of being, which is harmony, is a *feeling* that reflects into the mind as a diffusion of light.

"Now harmony is not a solitary thing. There must be, by the very definition of the word, something to be harmonious with. One cannot shut himself within, away from life, and attain this state. Nor is it more than a subterfuge to say that one is thus coming into harmony with an inner and spiritual world. The only effective way for an incarnated entity to touch a spiritual environment *must* be through the mechanisms in which he is placed. This does not decry the value of appropriate meditation. But meditation is appropriate only when it has gathered from external life—lived heartily—its own enwrapment. That is another subject; and I mention it here to forestall discussion.

"If these things are understood, I am going to tell you one thing flatly": he repeated his thesis, "in no life or circumstance of life are lacking the elements to supply adequately conditions of an harmonious state of being. This is true no matter how baffling, antagonistic, struggling one's condition of life and surroundings may be. Whatever the distress in the conscious mind, it still may, guided by the instincts of the heart, be led into contact with those elements of its earth environment with which it may move in its flowing contentment. Even to a prisoner in a barred cell comes some moment of the day when a shaft of sun through his bars, the tone of a distant bell, the faint murmur of a passing breeze offers a companionship which admitted, in its turn admits him for its brief moment to that state of being. And many more of these sparkle-moments are in the busier and varied days of those without the walls."

3.

If these premises are accepted, it follows inevitably that a man does not successfully go after happiness—harmony—either by accumulating things or by renouncing things. The problem is entirely where, within himself, he elects to dwell.

"If," said Gaelic, "one is able so to center the consciousness that his headquarters are within his own serenities, whatever they may be, then it follows that the hurries and clashes and struggles and potentially deterrent substances of life become an accompaniment and not an integral concomitant."

Our tool for this purpose is attention. We know that only by use of selection can we get along in everyday life. If we were forced to take conscious notice of every impression our senses actually receive, we should go crazy. Fortunately we are able to select what is appropriate to us, and ignore the rest. The instrument of selection is our choice in paying attention.

But, says Gaelic, that is the attention of the physical senses. It focusses by shutting out and ignoring. That sort of attention is a tool for use in the physical environment. It is a cold, sharp attention; which, indeed, is befitting to a tool.

But there is another type of attention, which concentrates by response, rather than by the shutting out characteristic of the physical powers. "It might," says Gaelic, "in contradistinction to the attention of the senses, be called the attention of the heart. What corresponds to the shutting out of the physical senses is a withdrawal of this warmth to its concentration upon its proper objects."

Its proper objects: that is important. Neither sort of attention works well in the other's field. If we take the center of our consciousness out from the harmony of our inner securities to apply it to matters that belong properly to the conscious mind, then it will be "jostled and pressed and suffering in those elements of life with which it should not have thus to do."

Unfortunately such ingredients of life are the most easily recognized. Sometimes we find them favorable and pleasant; sometimes disagreeable to the point of suffering. They are the necessary materials, the resistances, for that type of development we are to get by using the hard sharp tool of the intellect. So prominently are they in the forefront, and so closely do they press on us, that our tendency is to turn on them both kinds of attention—of the mind and the heart. Which, says Gaelic, results in "an anguished and unhappy existence."

"The objects to which we turn the deeper attention of the heart are not so easily apperceived," says he. "I say apperceived rather than recognized because, in ordinary diction, recognition implies the use of conscious intellect. This apperception is rather through the satisfied *feeling* of response. Once the apperception has taken place, however, often enough to have gained the further recognition of repeated response, it may penetrate or rise to the intellectual. The intellect, moreover, is valuable in making certain eliminations, definitions and placements, so that we may be placed more favorably for exposure, so to speak, to these deeper recognitions."

The functioning of life in this state of being we call harmony demands, says Gaelic, "no insistent haste or hurry. Its elements may move quickly; but if so, it is a quickness that is synchronized with our rhythm of the moment. Or, vice versa, their inpingement upon our day automatically and effortlessly quickens our rhythm to their own. In either case there is no *feeling* of undue haste, for these things must be of our serenities. In time, or rather in the widening spaces of our lives, more and more of these bits and phases of life peculiarly in affinity to our deeper selves touch elbows with us so often that we come to know consciously who and what they are; and later to search the crowds of our hours for their familiar faces. And when we have found one or more of them moving along with us in the weaving press, we fix our comfortable assurance on their familiar presence in this alien disorder through which, orderly, we must pass.

"Now let us repeat, with the new light of the preceding upon it, the statement that in every man's life, no matter how unhappy or suffering or full of anguished problems, there is a sufficiency for these companionships, perhaps muffled and veiled, but whose faces sometime in the past he has at least momentarily glimpsed, to bear him company, would he but call them around in his language of the heart. This, I repeat, is not an intellectual dissecting of life in search of what is sometimes piously called compensation. It is no silly, self-righteous and smirking 'look-upon-the-bright-side-of-things.' It is no avoidance of or thrusting aside that which affronts our steadfastness and courage. It is the recognition, by the heart, of our simple kinships; and the finding in them a sufficiency of companionship."

4.

When once, by experiencing the actual sensation, we have come into awareness of this inner basic harmony, we must safeguard it. It is easily invaded, dissolved, shattered by the din and confusion of life—if we permit. "This inner awareness must be guarded, as one steals moments from children's insistences to get adult refreshment. It is just that. The technique necessitates flexibility in turning from one consciousness to another, without irritations due to interruptions or tensions which come from unnatural spiritual straining. It must be a natural process. The child and adult analogy is good. The din of life is caused by the still childish consciousness of the race.

"The effort is to establish the awareness comfortably, in the beginning, without throwing it wide open to some kind of dangerous pacifism. It must be strong and durable and understandable, approached as refreshment and enjoyment, not as an acquisition-of-power exercise. Composure and a feeling of permanence is the idea."

It is, in a way, an inner citadel, a core of reality; our own, and not to be invaded.

"And yet," warned Gaelic impressively, "it must not be looked upon as a retiring place or refuge." Its possession is no excuse for drawing aside from life's disagreeable agitations, merely because they are disagreeable, and it is possible thus to avoid them. "The difficulty in taking such shelter is not that it is inefficient, for it is possible to rise to such a consciousness that your skirts are unwet by the storm; but that, when again you stick out your head, the world may have passed you by. You must take your full share of the buffeting of the elements.

"Like a ship on the waters you move forward in a serene unconcern, knowing full well that your habitation is secure, but with a share in the toward movement. Those who have not built their habitations, their stability, may by the storm be shaken into an acknowledgment that such habitations are desirable. It is by the buffeting of a time like this that men discover their own reliances. If the spark is in them, they must begin to search. Those who have already acknowledgedly constructed a stability have now an opportunity, otherwise lacking, of testing its integrity and of learning that mere escape is sterile. Beware lest you join the escapists."

"On the other hand," he continued, "times of especial stress do not mean that you are called upon to plunge heedless into the muck and mire. You must do what is offered to your hand; but it is no more desirable now that you cripple your wings by seizing more than your power can lift than in times of contentment. Do what comes, bear what comes in natural course, but do not overweight beyond what your serenity is capable of floating. Distinguish between withdrawal and hearty but undamaged living. It is a time of trial; but times of trial are also times of readjustment and movement. It is not an arbitrary redistribution, but rather an allowing of each thing to settle to its own specific gravity. Uncomfortable, distressful, if you have not your own up-bearing vehicle of consciousness; stimulating and forwarding of the Scheme, if you have."

"I am so often puzzled," said one of us, "to decide what I ought to tackle; what channels in the outer world are intended for me. I don't want to make a mistake."

"They rarely come labelled," replied Gaelic. "You refuse to

take what comes merely because you are not absolutely sure. If you timidly wait, your own may pass you unrecognized. There is always the back track. A frankness in admitting that you are 'off on the wrong foot' effectively undoes mistake. Do not be afraid to test what is brought to you. If you shrink because of a sense of doubt, you are entering the realms of fear. If you cannot *set* your timid judgment aside, step aside *from* it. We are not dependent enough on the interpenetration of all things in cosmos. We treat each thing separately. Storms are a test of your seaworthiness. They are not 'sent as a test,' but come in the usual course of cause and effect. In suffering one can acquire impetus, dynamics. Serenity is a feeling that things matter only in your relationship to them.

"These admonitions," he concluded, "may seem to you at first mystic, somewhat vague, and not made up of sufficient importances. They are not intended as a formula; but rather as a direction toward growth."

CHAPTER X.

The Sequence of Creation

1.

Such, in broad principle, is the meaning of our Job—whatever it is; our equipment for the Job; our attitude toward it; our aids to accomplishing it. Remains only to learn how to do it, what methods to use in approaching and tackling it.

All jobs are accomplished by the same basic methods, said Gaelic. They are a creative process: exactly the same sequence that brings into being a picture or a poem or a symphony is necessary to bring into being an automobile, or a new industrial combination, or an ordered government of oneself or others. Exactly the same sequence has brought into being the tiny world we live in and the enormous galaxies of incomprehensible space. And in the sense that art is a creative process, all of life is art, all evolution is art. So if we are to seek for an inclusive method, by which any job whatever may be done, we must examine the method by which a true artist attains his results, and what happens to him in the process. How, exactly, does he go about his picture or his symphony or his poem?

He "creates" it, we say. Well, what is "creation"? In general it is the making of something in cosmos that has not been there before. In universal undifferentiated space and force, uniformity is broken. There is initiated in that uniformity a stress point, a vortex, and the universal substance there ceases to be force and becomes matter. The precise point where this happens eludes science as yet, though science has pursued the constituents of matter through molecule, atom, proton, electron across the border into pure force.

2.

This pure force Gaelic postulates as a higher undifferentiated flow or universal spiritual substance—or Presence of God in the finite. This concept will be recognized. Bergson expresses it in another way in his *élan vital*. It is the primordial stream of vitality, of life. The Source. It flows "ceaselessly through all cosmos," says he. "It becomes evident only when arrested, or rather slowed up, when it becomes either visible or palpable or effective, through the effort of its dynamics to free itself and proceed upon its way."

How and by what is it arrested, or slowed up? By an idea; or by a purpose: both necessarily originated by Intelligence. Intelligence is the refracting prism, so to speak.

"Arrested by an *idea* it becomes a creature or a thing, dependent for its form and its attributes upon the nature of the idea; what you have called the quality of consciousness. Slowed up by a *purpose*, rather than an idea, it becomes a vehicle of differentiated force, dependent for its nature and its effect upon the nature of the purpose."

Idea and purpose are attributes of intelligence. The underlying reality of cosmos is Intelligence, an All-Consciousness which is infinite, and which we, as finite minds, cannot understand. Necessarily finite creation must be part of this consciousness, of its same stuff. But it is what it is because of its underlying Idea. A dog is a dog, with a dog's form and attributes and limitations, because of the peculiar quality of consciousness he possesses, and which forms and animates him. He is essentially the same thing as everything else. That is to say, his consciousness is part of the All-Consciousness; and his body is made up of proton and electron. What molds and limits those common things into a dog, is Idea—his *dogness*.

Similarly, Consciousness assumes the form of a tree, rather than any other, because of its essential *treeness*. And so with all individual things. Life, as life, is obviously a single animating vitality. It expresses itself through the enormous variety of its forms simply because of an equal variety of qualities, of Ideas, in universal consciousness.

Since this is so, it follows that, in undifferentiated universal substance, the potentiality for any kind of creation is everywhere present. Then why a tree here, a rock there, and a dog somewhere else? What governs their appearance at that precise "pin point of space"? Is it, we surmised, because at that point the tree quality is stronger than other qualities?

Not exactly, replied Gaelic; rather it is because at that place the *conditions* are better for the manifestation of treeness than for the manifestation of any other quality.

That was reasonable; but, like many explanations, it merely pushed the question back. Why are the conditions better at that particular place? How is that law made to work?

The law is not made to work, stated Gaelic; no one ever makes a law work. We demurred.

"No man makes a law work," he repeated, "he merely assembles in proper juxtaposition and proportion the necessary conditions. Having done so, he cannot *prevent* the law from acting. You think you light the fire. As a matter of fact, you pile your wood, you place your kindling, you insert the paper. You then supply the chemical, under those conditions of motion and abrasion necessary to the oxygenation of those materials. The law steps in."

We acknowledged the distinction.

You use intelligence in supplying the conditions, Gaelic extended the argument.

"Who or what gathers together in like manner the conditions necessary to the production or manifestation of your tree quality or whatever-quality?" he challenged. "The same thing in essence which has gathered together the fire material—*Intelligence*.

"There is no working of any law unless the conditions for that law are arranged. And that arrangement comes through Intelligence.

"You may—would ye quibble—point to the gathering of certain conditions by the action of certain laws, but that is only pushing the subject back. In the final analysis you will still discover—Intelligence."

3.

Creation then, Gaelic summed it up, whether of a universe or a poem or a way of life, is all the same in process. It is simply a checking at one point of the flow of universal Harmony; its differentiation into various elements; and the arrangement of these elements into form. The checking is done by the will of an individual intelligence; the rearrangement is made by an Idea of that intelligence; the manifestation of that Idea is accomplished by assembling the conditions for its embodiment, again by intelligence. The resultant form is the artistic creation.

There are, said Gaelic, several corollaries to consider.

The amount of force that an individual may be able to check is determined by his capacity. His capacity, in turn, depends on his degree of development.

His ability to rearrange into form is measured by his innate creative imagination—his talent or genius.

The endurance of the form, its "life expectation," is measured by the dynamics its creator put into it. The dynamics are generated by the intensity of his spiritual development and aspiration.

There is the sequence. It is an invariable sequence, says Gaelic, of any creation, great or small. The thing is "real," as we call it, and not merely a fancy, because both the preliminary fashioning by imagination "in the substance of thought" and the later embodiment in material take place in a finite medium. "I use the word finite in place of material," says Gaelic, "though in a broad sense the two terms are interchangeable. However, common acceptance has given the word material a narrower connotation."

4.

Now we are ready to examine into the processes of the artist in factual detail. How does he make his start on his statue or his ode? What does he *do?* What *must* he do?

"First of all," says Gaelic, "the creative intelligence must place himself in the current of cosmic harmony. This is a voluntary spiritual act. We may call it by various names—receptivity, openness to inspiration, and the like. It is, however, nothing so specific as receptivity to detail, but rather a spiritual attitude and altitude."

This is the origin and source of what we call his "inspiration," and of which we stand in awe as something peculiar to "genius." We think it is not for us commonplace folk less richly endowed. But it *is* for us, as we shall see.

"Inspiration," continues Gaelic, "is not a suggestion of detail ready formed. It is a pouring in of all essence in a vital stream, from which the creator segregates and absorbs those things appropriate to his vision, as the organs and functioning mechanisms and tissues of the body take from the homogeneous blood stream those elements, and those elements only, which make for their health and building. That is why a considered reaching up the stream toward the source, in a conscious grasping for what has been intellectually desired, is futile, or even destructive. The mechanism of recognition, segregation and absorption lies lower down in the wholeness of the human organism.

"Now this receptivity is not a mere opening of the door, as one opens the gates of a dam. You must recall that I said that the very first requisite was to *place* oneself in the current; and that means not an opening, but a definite effort of aspiration."

There must be as yet no effort to "think things out," warned Gaelic. That is not the approach for creation; only for hack work. There is no place here for the intellect. It will have its innings, in due time, but that is later. Intellectual reaching is a grasping for definite and defined detail, the alleged need for which has been conceived by the intellect itself, which at this stage knows nothing of what it needs. Again analogously to the selection by the various tissues of the body from the blood stream, the creative faculty selects for itself those harmonies and those racially created fashionings which its genius builds into the elements of its new vision of creation.

"That is the forming of the mold. As it is a process of assimilation and reproduction, the delicacy of its development requires the comforting enwrapment of time and of brooding cherishing. Until the hour of its unfoldment its petals must not be pried apart by the sharp fingers of intellect, nor forced by the hot breathing of haste. It must be allowed its due and graceful period of gestation before it can be brought forth for handling. It must be allowed to lie quiet, warmed by, one might say, a sort of suspended and reverent attention."

This is the period of aspiration. Aspiration is a spiritual effort. It is a quality, not an action. Whether or not the artist is fully conscious of what is going on makes no difference. That, says Gaelic, is a matter of individual constitution. "Some have no consciousness of it at all. Inspiration visits them unexpected, and apparently unsummoned. Others go so far as to place themselves in an attitude of attunement. Still others have some formula, simple or elaborate; and the rarer mystics of high development realize exactly what is forward. Sometimes the illusion of attunement or the lip service of the formula fails to produce the actual rising to the necessary spiritual height. In that case, since the person is not actually in the current, inspiration cannot flow in."

5.

That is the first and absolutely essential period of conception and gestation. It lies in the realm of pure imaginative inspiration. It has not yet clothed itself in the form of details. The artist has not yet come to think about them, to consider what they must be, or how they must be put together for external embodiment. Before the conception can rise into visibility it must have shape, color, words, tones, harmonies. These must be found and selected and arranged by the artist. For this purpose he now, for the first time, begins consciously to use his intellect.

Nevertheless, if he stopped right there, in the mere disembodied conception, he would have accomplished something. "For now there is," says Gaelic, "an assembling of already existent elements in a novel arrangement expressing an advance in spiritual content." That novel arrangement now exists in the substance of thought. It is something; and if circumstance cuts short the sequence right there, the effort has not been fruitless. Nevertheless, says Gaelic, "the artist is not justified in merely composing his work subjectively, no matter how completely carried out the composition. To be sure, he has by that action drawn together in new arrangement to the establishment of a possibility. It exists as a possibility which did not have previous existence; a possibility which may advantage, as material, another with sufficient perception to perceive and respond to it. That is so much to the good. But it is not established as a mold in cosmos until its outline has been surrounded and defined by a definite outward manifestation, accomplished by an exercise of that kind of productive faculty with which the artist is endowed."

Without that "assurance of integrity by means of manifestation" the mere conception goes little beyond day-dreaming.

This "manifestation"—the book, or picture, or symphony—requires an intelligent ordering of materials, which means the use of the intellect. But not, as yet, use of the intellect exclusively. The man who deliberately selects, plans, and constructs, as he would tackle a cross-word puzzle, is a hack: an artisan, not an artist. He is to make selection of the materials he will use; but that selection will not be from the whole universe of possible materials. He is not to suffer so much bewilderment. His choice is to be only from those materials brought within his reach by the magnetic quality of his vision.

That happy short-cut is possible to him, however, only if he continues, as he has begun, to work in the intuitive regions of his mind.

"Besides this attitude of spiritual receptivity (*i.e.*, the inspiration-gestation period)," said Gaelic, "is also one which is closely akin, closely analogous, but different in exact kind. One may call it, for this purpose, a psychic receptivity. In it one lays his hands upon the fashioned materials which he will employ in his arrangement. They must be received through an open heart; for the whole substance of harmony is the vibration in sympathy. That which is antipathetic is also a dissonance. The vision which forms within oneself is a compound of these two sorts of receptivity, molded and determined by individual genius and affinity.

"During that period, from that second stream of inspiration, which we call psychic, details apparently isolated and unattached will float to the artist's concept almost at random, until at last it stands ready for the intellectual fashioning. That is the second step of the process. It does not come to you, if you have not placed yourself in the stream.

"You have already been told," reminded he, "that a mere opening to receptivity is not enough; that you must make the spiritual effort to *step* into the flow. Once open to, once within the sweep of All-Consciousness, those things pertinent may be appropriated to your purpose.

"Your necessity of selection is narrowed by the magnetic affinity of your underlying intention; so that within the radius of your grasp are attracted, by that affinity, those matters which are applicable; and are deflected, by the opposed polarity, those things which have no appositiveness."

If this were permitted to work exactly according to the blue print, then, the artist could be sure—provided he held himself "in the flow"—that anything that then suggested itself to him would be appropriate material. But that, Gaelic pointed out, would mean a perfect vision, an absolutely clear intention, a pure aim. And the artist is human!

"Unfortunately this unadulterated purity cannot be expected from an organism as complex, and as partially in control, as the human entity in its present state of development. Subsidiary and untimely cross-purposes, perhaps imperfect, perhaps merely misplaced to the occasion, cannot be entirely eliminated. They also attract their apposites, so that the artist is left selection, not only from super-abundance, but from the inappropriate.

"The richness of material swept by the current within reach depends on the displacement of the spiritual body of yourself that you plant within the stream. The eddies resultant are wider or smaller in scope, circle wider and more inclusively, according to the bulk and weight that is the containment of your degree. The swirl of the small man has but small extent and power, and can deflect to attraction but few imponderables, with which he must build but an airy miniature of structure. Nevertheless if he has worked in sincerity throughout, it will be a true and acceptable creation."

The artistic "sense," "gift," "genius"—whatever one pleases to call it—is largely the ability to distinguish what material belongs by affinity to the vision, and what is swept within reach by the "cross-purposes." Even one most unskilled mechanically, but who has artistic sense, says Gaelic, "is able to distinguish—when the time of distinguishment arrives—between that which is drawn in affinity to his central concept, and that which drifts in answer to the unsubduable or unsubdued adulterations of other purpose. So that one would not attach the tail of a fish, however beautiful in itself, to his picture of his dog. But the exact appropriateness of that which is drawn to the call of the central concept is dependent, not upon the strength of desire, or ambition to accomplish, or upon a realization of need, but solely upon the steadfast purity of the intention.

"And, per contra, if the artist entertains the calmness of spiritual conviction that his intention is pure, then whatever presents itself for his creative consideration, he may rest assured, is proper material. No matter how ill-favored, or dissonant, or even destructive it may at first glance appear. It would be such only if attracted to a flickering or wavering central concept. Though darkness may be the cold containment of death, yet you would use its shadow to fill the supporting hollows in the nobility of your design."

"Pretty difficult!" said we doubtfully. "How can one tell?"

Gaelic agreed.

"The only criterion you can put to yourself as to what I called the purity of original intention," said he, "is not an intellectual examination of motive, but an orientation of inner being toward a hunger or desire to produce something, comprised within the limitations of the present project, that shall be an expression of ultimate harmony."

6.

Gaelic seemed most anxious to impress on us that stopping short of some sort of material embodiment is always incompletion. He deprecated strongly the school that emphasizes the "inner life" and is satisfied to devote itself solely to its development. "The well-meaning person, filled with sweetness and light and higher resolve, who places himself as a luminary in the heavens to spread abroad an *abstraction* of beautiful harmony wherewith to saccharinize circumambience, accomplishes just the sum total of nothing!" said he. *"In the finite one cannot create with abstraction, but only through a medium.* One must definitely work out his pattern of creation through some sort of medium. Without the inertia and resistance of a medium, dynamics lack, and the pattern is devoid of stability, or persistence and endurance."

Betty a little objected to this. "It seems to me," she writes in annotation, "some people have the job of working in abstractions, 'harmony patterns,' preparing available material for the people of action. I do not like the swat at dreamers." That is true; but I think Gaelic means the creation is not *finished* until it is embodied. Gaelic intended no swat. There has been actual accomplishment in the substance of thought to be sure. Something new has been created in cosmos. Occasionally it happens that circumstance cuts down the original artist short of completion. Nevertheless he has accomplished; for there now exists what Gaelic called a "mold" which another may fill. But filled it must be before it takes on the stability of a created thing.

7.

So far, I think, anyone who has ever dabbled in the arts will recognize the sequence which Gaelic has outlined. But the matter goes beyond the formal arts. Gaelic used the artist merely as an easy example of a general process which operates through all life's activities. The engineer, industrialist, statesman, business executive takes exactly the same steps, whether he knows it or not. Many of them do know it, and will acknowledge that their best solutions, when they are up against the knots in their problems, come to them "in a flash when they are thinking about something else," or in their sleep overnight, or "on hunch," or in some other indirect way of inspiration.

8.

That would seem to end the discussion. We have the artist, and his process, and finally his fashioned embodiment of the vision of his inspiration. He holds the objective thing in his hand, a material embodiment or expression of an arrangement of harmonies that did not before exist. That is Gaelic's definition. It would seem that he had finished with that job and could go on to the next. He cannot do so, says Gaelic, if he is to make of it a completed creation. It does exist; but the purpose of a thing is not mere existence. It must *be*. And it cannot be said to *be* until it functions. Imagine someone, with the knowledge and the materials, building an engine in the depths of some far-off jungle. It might be a fine and creditable structure; an object of interest and curiosity to the natives; but it could hardly be considered an *engine*—a thing to accomplish something—until it is placed where it will work. In other words, function. To function it must do more than just exist; it must come into relationship.

That is true also of your pure artist. He is driven by a strong impulse to share his production; an impulse that runs deeper than personal ambition. Personal ambition is merely a powerful promoting stimulus toward the more secret end. This may be seen in cases of genuine anonymity. No one can doubt the artist's choice, were choice given between showing without his name, or not showing at all.

The impulse to share, says Gaelic, is infused through all ordinary living. "So deep-founded is it that often the mere facing alone of a beautiful object carries with it an almost aching sense of incompletion."

I think we have all felt that ache, that desire to have someone with us to share our emotion, endorse it so to speak, when alone we have blundered upon an especially beautiful sunset, say.

This, says Gaelic, is "peculiarly a necessity in the case of the original creative artist. It is useless to make your form and hide it in a crypt. It must be placed within the eye of appreciation to draw to itself its containing affirmment. That function is very analogous to the original placing in receptivity of the artist's own consciousness in fructifying his intention. It is not sufficient to withdraw the veil and stand aside in expectation of the chance passer-by. It must be carried in joyful outheld hands, with the same eagerness of spirit, intent on sharing a new-found treasure, as that with which one runs from the fields flower-laden, avid to display his garnering.

"There is a fine line here to be drawn; the line that divides offering from demanding. You offer to attention; you cannot demand it. Nevertheless, this distinction does not absolve you from holding before one, and another, and another in turn your fashioning, in test of recognition. You cannot sit, cowled and silent, in the obscurity of the market corner, torpid in a dumb faith that a time is appointed when one shall come.

"The area of legitimate search for the outlet to the necessary appreciation is like the circle of individual responsibility. Within that circle dwells not only the absolute right, but the duty of search. Within that circle swarm those unheeding, whose affinities do not vibrate to this occasion. Their attention may be called; but only by a great shout that shall startle them from their legitimate business. Among them you walk softly, and offer in silence, testing for the spark of recognition. You may utter your shout, an ye will, and you may call all eyes to you; and, if your words be cunning, you may sell your ware. But you have stepped beyond the obligation of your sharing, and that which replies back is a crumbling doubt which makes no permanence.

"Nevertheless, because you see some that so shout their wares, pressing here and there until the whole world seems full of their insistences, that does not lift from you, on the risings of your disgust, the duty of moving in seemly dignity about your proper searchings. Until you have found the pedestal and placed upon it the work of your hands; until you have situated it upon the fair pleasaunces where walk those whose eyes it can pleasure, then is your work as little deserving of your signature as though you had abandoned it rough-buried in the clay.

"You may not leave the children of your begetting upon the river bank, nor rest your searching until they are bestowed."

CHAPTER XI.

Appreciation and Repetition

1.

Such is Gaelic's conception of the individual artist, and what he accomplishes in creation. He has made a new arrangement of harmony; in the world of ideas, of the substance of thought, he has constructed a mold; the mold, when filled with the material substance of embodiment, has become the Thing created. Furthermore even if the object itself be destroyed, the arrangement of harmony still exists to be of further use in embodiments; the mold is there for refilling. To the manner of its refilling we shall shortly return, but now it is simpler to stick to the direct argument.

However, says Gaelic, the mold is not necessarily permanent, nor even very long-lived in and of itself. It can dissolve. As a mold it must be consolidated, made firm and enduring. For this two things are necessary—appreciation and repetition. It must have its audience; and it must be repeated. So here the art of creation ceases to be solitary. We the people furnish our indispensable contribution.

2.

For, Gaelic points out, everything must first be constructed in the substance of thought before it can be precipitated in manifestation. And further, a thing does not even then really exist without that filtration through consciousness that we call appreciation. Unthinking we accept the common idea that spiritual quality, such as beauty, is inherent in certain combinations of physical things; that such a combination is, per se, beautiful whether "anybody sees them or not." That is only partially true, says Gaelic; and he proves it by a striking statement:

"Spiritual qualities in general are not *things*, but *responses*." Without someone to respond, they do not function.

"You have all known and appreciated the natural beauty of, for example, the great spaces of your desert lands," he illustrated. "You know the wide fling of their shimmering expanses, the tinted veils of their evening lights, and the brooding magic that distills from their presence before you, as a perfume from a flower. Those emotions and esthetic appreciations filter through your consciousness and become a portion of the awareness existing in the universal consciousness.

"But consider the same desert before the advent of one capable of such appreciation. The stark material embodiment was always there, the wide expanses, the uplifting mountains, the gray sage, the white dry alkali, the shimmer of heat waves, the shadow of cloud. All lay existent in stark materiality then as now. One thing only lacked in full measure; and that is beauty. To such creatures as inhabited the waste its appearances corresponded solely with the response equipment of their kind. The lizard felt the warmth or the cold; became cognizant in its own way of such elements of its environment as suited its simple life—no more. The beasts that roamed its plains saw each its own world in which veils of sunset, inspiration of shadow, appeal of space, of sun and mountain did not exist, except as such things represented material facts in their lives. The savage also, while a little more completely aware, still fell short of supplying, through his appreciation, the spirit of beauty which broods over those lands.

"Beauty exists there only when an appropriate response

evolves it into the substance of thought. The many passed
that way unseeing, wrapped in the discomfort of dust, of daily
toil, of thirst, and hunger and fatigue, and saw in it only a
hinderment to travel and a labor to be overcome. The many
would so continue to have passed were it not that someone
among them, at some time, brought there the out-reaching
spirit of appreciation, and so for the first time introduced there
beauty."

Though his illustration dealt only with the one quality of
beauty, Gaelic gave us to understand that the principle is universal. There must be this echo-back from consciousness before the substance of the dream has reality, and before the
mold of harmony can be made available for general use, so
to speak. Appreciation is as definite a contribution to whole
creation as any of the other qualities which seem to us the
peculiar property of genius. Appreciation too works in the
substance of thought, and therefore joins hands as co-worker
with the original creative impulse.

3.

That is where we, the ordinary citizens, come in most definitely
not only as co-partners, but as absolutely necessary co-partners.
That is why there must be an audience; why the artist so
urgently seeks the showing. The audience is not merely for
glorification and applause. It is not a bystander; it operates an
actual creative function.

"Each act of conscious appreciation, no matter how small,"
insists Gaelic, "creates definitely a reality in cosmos, or else
strengthens a reality already existent, by which it is easier for
similar manifestations to take place. If this is a wholly new
mechanism, one that has not heretofore been employed, the
act (of appreciation) is as solid a movement in evolution as
is the appearance of a new form, or a modification, in the
physical world."

So necessary an ingredient is sharing that even in ordinary life we get little satisfaction from a discovery in book or picture or play or movie unless we pass it on to a friend or two. Our impulse is to share our pleasure. That is what we think, but it is more than that, says Gaelic: actually we are obeying a profound instinct.

"We are extending the possibility of the consolidating force which makes for endurance; are adding another lamina toward making permanent the mold.

"So our discovery of whatever appeals to our responsive sense brings with it a responsibility to pass on the opportunity for the utilization of others."

That is an important function, but we can do even better. We may actually ourselves become interpretative artists, though we would certainly not label ourselves as such. But Gaelic does.

"It may be that occasionally some chance of angle or fall of light makes ours the only eye to see. There is in such cases laid upon us also the duty of interpretative creation that will shift the concept upon the visibility powers of others. Interpretative creation is thus a very high form of art, in that it implies a sympathetic understanding of the original artist's manifested intention; a clear-eyed understanding of one's own angle of view; and an intuitive understanding of the angles of view of one's fellow men. These can be no inconsiderable endowments."

4.

"So," Gaelic once more summed up, "we have the creative gathering and arrangement; the outward clothing in manifestation; and the repercussion back of the appreciative quality. There remains still one other necessary element to the wholly efficient working of this new thing in the world. It must, for its fullest use and effect, receive the solidifying influence of repetition.

"Each repetition of outward manifestation adds to the mold, so to speak, another microscopic lamina of containment. The mold gains strength and substance by use. This is the accrued value that inheres in the older created compositions that have stood the test of time on their authenticity as products of true creative imagination—the ratio of increasing influence.

"There is one distinction to be made. Repetition need not in all forms of art be repetition of too definite an outward seeming. It may be a repetition of the inner creative conception. It might avail little to copy repeatedly the outlines and color and tones of a particular picture. It avails much to repeat the inner vision that inspired it. A work of literature is repeated literally, of course, through its numerous copies, reaching thus its appreciation. But particularly in the realm of music the distinction obtains, for right here comes in the value of the interpretative artist. Through his individual rendition he is able to avoid the brittle hardening of the mold consequent on mere literal copying; and to contribute that flexible freshener of interpretation which will preserve its integrity.

"These four processes constitute the full cycle of artistic creation, though the word *artistic* could well be elided. All true creation is an effort of art."

CHAPTER XII.

Creative Intelligence

1.

IN COMPACT review, then, the sequence of process to embody the artistic vision is as follows:

The checking of the universal flow. This is done by intelligence.

The rearrangement of already existing conditions into a new harmony. That makes a "mold in the substance of thought."

The mold is filled with the appropriate material substance to the production of the Thing-Created.

The permanence of the mold for future refilling, so to say, is assured by appreciation and repetition.

That is the method of the artist. It is also the process by which all things in the finite universe are brought into being.

2.

All things, Gaelic emphasized, "*Any manifestation whatever is an effort of creative intelligence.*"

"Hold on!" we objected. "That statement takes in a lot of territory—do you mean everything we can see, hear, touch, smell—"

"—or in any other way perceive," he finished the sentence for us.

"In the broad way of divine creation, yes—" we conceded doubtfully. But that, as we suspected, was not what Gaelic meant. He was talking of the individual intelligence much nearer home.

"Do you mean to say," someone objected, "that some invisible artist or other sat down and designed that sunset we saw last night?"

"Or those fancy tropical fish in the aquarium?" this from another.

"Or the exquisite flowers in the garden?"

In a way, said Gaelic; but perhaps not literally in the manner we seemed to imply. Somebody originally designed the particular balance of harmony back of these things.

"The idea comes first," he reminded. "The outward expression follows upon an inward creative fashioning. And that— wherever and however you find it—is first, a tuning into the universal power; and then a 'stepping down' of that power into the degree that will manifest."

That concept was already familiar enough. His next statement was arresting.

"The flower in the garden," he took one of our own examples, "is in last analysis an indication that an intelligence has, with creative effort, to the degree of that flower's perfection, succeeded in seizing upon and identifying itself with a portion of universal harmony.

"A mold of that arrangement of harmony has been made and filled."

We shook our heads a little over the notion of someone assigned in cosmos to designing flowers. It sounded like china painting. But our conclusions proved to be too hasty.

"That the *manifestation* has taken the form of a flower," said Gaelic, "does not necessarily mean that the originating creative intelligence has designed and constructed a flower. It may be that, in another medium, it has given voice and form to music, setting thus in motion dynamic circumscribed bits of creative harmony, which, carrying over into this earth medium, and encountering conditions favorable for that manifestation, produces itself as the colorful perfumed notes of a garden. And, vice versa, the music which one, in his best creative mood, has harmonized into creative vibrational bits, may well manifest itself over here in a pattern of color, conveying the same esthetic satisfaction in the one case as in the other."

In that thought, Gaelic interrupted the main thread of his argument to interpolate, lies the encouragement to those who strive apparently without recognition. Their efforts seem futile, but the futility is only seeming.

"It is the principle that lies back of the creative power of thought; though that is to some extent a misnomer. The creative power of fashioning imagination would be better. Whatever is so fashioned clothes itself—somewhere and somehow; now or later—in outward manifestation simply because it has been given form and, like a mold, exists now where it did not exist before, capacious to be filled when conditions supply the materials for that filling. In this sense, therefore, *no genuine creative effort is ever lost*. It has produced a phase of harmony which has not existed in exactly that form before. It has added to the harmonious differentiation of the universe detailed bits that have heretofore had no existence. As we see it now, the circle in whatever is the inunderstandable purpose will be rounded only when all potentiality is brought forth consciously and made evident. Furthermore, the potentiality itself is the intelligent creative act of the Great Originator.

"There are two small corollaries to add to this concept," resumed his thesis. "The first is that no genuine creation is without result. A mold may be placed upon a shelf awaiting the molten in due time. But the shape exists in the universe where existence it had not had before. Its eternal quality is not limited by the small manifestation of form which may at one time be made by its means. The mold is intact for the uses of harmony at its need.

"The second corollary is that intelligence does not create harmony, but comes into attunement with harmony, which it can utilize only according to the power of its will to achieve.

"So we observe that manifestation in the finite of the unbroken unmanifested infinite is an arresting for the purpose of visibility, so to speak, by creative intelligence. Intelligence so works only by conscious act of will. The act of creation is the setting in motion of a specific set of vibrations. That set of vibrations clothes itself in form according to the medium in which it is expressed. If its dynamics are sufficiently powerful, it may carry beyond its first medium of expression into other and different media; in which case the form of manifestation may be different. But it will be the same in power and degree of harmony.

"You mentioned a sunset as a beautiful thing remote from the possibility of actual personal designing. The conception of a gigantic artist with a gigantic palette and brush is indeed incredible to you. When you call from your recollection a particularly gorgeous and symmetrically balanced sunset painted across the sky, your poetic mood may have caused you to exclaim, 'What a master designer has limned the picture!' But you would have said it with no thought of its being a literal truth. Nevertheless, no balance of structure in the design, no contrast or blending of harmony of color, no gradation of tone, but has actually sometime been created by a designing intelligence. Nor could it there be present if an intelligence had not operated. That statement is literally true. And yet, if you therefore figure to yourself an artist planning out and fixing in the pigments of the skies the picture you see before you, you will be wrong. No intelligence, as far as we know, has the power to assemble those celestial phenomena to produce that exact thing. Nor does it necessarily mean that somewhere some artist has conceived or arranged the exact pattern and design you so much admire. But it does mean that somewhere, working in his *own* medium, some intelligence has creatively conceived a certain just and balanced arrangement of harmony which, *expressed in sunset,* produces this particular spectacle."

It happened that we had, that day, been examining a book called *Art Forms in Nature,* a collection of micro-photographs, and had been struck by the resemblance of many of them to modern architecture.

"You have today," continued Gaelic, "looked in a tome wherein are pictures of marvellously beautiful, though microscopic, columns and scrolls and arabesques and spearheads and many others, which, if designed and placed on paper by a pictorial or achitectural artist would arouse your admiration. Their balance and symmetry seem to exceed sometimes the best efforts of those artists. You exclaim, perhaps, in wonder over the marvellous artistry of nature, or perhaps of God, if you are theologically inclined. Nevertheless, each one of those forms is a result of careful and inspired design by an intelligent artist. This statement is not nullified by the probable fact that the originating intelligence had no such forms in mind. He had produced, stripped from clothing in *any* form of manifestation, and considered in its pure abstraction, a harmonious arrangement heretofore non-existent. Now in his approach to that creation it mattered not whether he set out to draw the design for a seed or a cathedral or a symphony or a color arrangement or a poem. That depended upon the personal idiosyncrasy of his genius, or his opportunity. The medium was only the resistance necessary to the dynamics of his conception. The conception itself is the true object, whether he knows it or not. If the poem or the symphony were all, as he thinks, there would be only that one small material thing added to the treasure of the universe. But the creation of a new harmony pattern makes a possible seed pod, cathedral, symphony, painting, poem, and all other things of beauty that vibrate to it.

"You were speculating today," he continued, "whether the man might have obtained his architectural inspiration for his lofty building from the minute plant stalk. If he had known of it! As far as the resemblance holds in beauty he did so. But not by reference to the miscroscope, but through the vibration of affinity to the original harmony arrangement from which both sprang."

An object of art—such as the painting or symphony or whatnot—is ordinarily the work of one man. His is the genius and the technical judgment and skill that has conceived the vision, fostered it to wholeness, and precipitated it in embodiment. But when we deal with the more complicated larger evolutions —which Gaelic still regards as works of art—the process is not always so easily discerned. The group effort may be necessary; the job is too big for one individual. And therefore often we see the dream apparently futile and the dreamer forgotten, but nevertheless the vision itself later embodied by another who gets the credit. Gaelic speaks a word for the unrecognized, and also for healthy balance against too loud acclaim for easy success. "Creative genius," Gaelic reminded, "is composed of two actions. The conception of a thing must first be made in the substance of thought; and then precipitated in manifestation on the physical plane. These may be combined in one individual, so that a man both conceives his vision and embodies it. Or of these two actions each may find its embodiment in a different individual. Then, in appearance, you have the spectacle of one who struggles frustrated throughout his life, without arrival at the world's success. You have on the other hand the spectacle of one producing abundantly and beautifully, almost as it were by instinct, without labor, almost without taking thought, a child of good fortune. One is condemned as a failure: the other is almost revered in his success. Nevertheless, often the first, the failure, has made true his vision; and the other, the genius, has done no more than possess the open eye wherewith to see, and the hand wherewith, unknowing to his own soul, to pass on.

"The measure of progress is not always the work of the hand, but is often the inner fashioning."

3.

Gaelic had defined the role of appreciation in the creation of the work of art. It is just as necessary to the wholeness of every-day living, exercised "as regularly and easily as the breath is drawn. We will now," says Gaelic, "extend the conception to a man's daily environment. Each item of detail in that environment is a product of creative fashioning, brought into being in no manner differently than is the painting, the poem, or the musical composition. It is the filling, by material manifestation, of the mold formed in the substance of thought by the creative intention of intelligence. Its eternal assurance depends, not on this material manifestation which perishes and passes, but upon the solid integrity of the mold that outlines the intention. That, as we have elsewhere explained, is contributed to by response—the response of understanding appreciation. I speak literally when I say that he who in passing notes with sympathetic and pleasured eyes the sheen of light upon the wayside flower, has not merely pleased his own esthetic sense, but has made a small but definite contribution to whatever intention has brought it about.

"The deliberate, conscious, seeking appreciation of all by which you are surrounded and of all that life encounters, is more than a pleasurable functioning: it is an opportunity of contribution. It, so to speak, assists in repairing the wear of the mold, and in preserving it pristine for further manifestation.

"But it has more of a reciprocal action than you would at first perceive. *Life in consciousness is not a state of being, but a response,*" he thought it worth while to repeat and expand this thought. "Without any response whatever, there can be no life. That is instinctively well understood; as is well evidenced by the figure of speech you use when you say that 'so-and-so is dead to the world of music or of beauty or of what-not.' You mean that he has no response for them. So in your filling of your moments with appreciation you are receiving back from them more life.

"You are surrounded by so many possible response-mechanisms that, if you opened your consciousness to them indiscriminately, nought but confusion could result. So you have the power of opening your attention, or of closing it down, as you draw the jalousies of a window. So easily is this done, and so gratefully does the laziness of your attention bask in the darkness, that a bad habit is easily acquired of walking through your daily affairs from point to point of your necessities, veiled. On either side as you walk are the wee small unimportant beauties of fashionings created by the long slow processes which you know. Each is the wonderful and delicate flowering of the slow deep toil of intelligent intention. Each offers silently the gift it has for your spirit; and beseeches silently the waters for which it thirsts, and which response to its intention alone can supply. You may withdraw and withhold if you will: but to loss. I say 'loss,' and not 'your loss' or 'its loss.' I say loss: of a possibility, small mayhap, but a loss none the less of what should be the fullness of the cosmic functioning.

"So I tell you, walk not shrouded; but look ye to right and left in open eye and heart, as a prince taking his ease, avid to receive and return his loyalties. You may take pleasure in your esthetic sense of the harmonies you perceive; you may also permit yourself a small glow of satisfaction that you are, in your small way, fulfilling, performing a definite function of the whole purpose.

"In our larger moments, with concentration of our powers, we trace our bit of the pattern as it is revealed to us; but in our smaller moments, without effort, with pleasure, we may also be working effectively, both to ourselves and the Intention, in the substance of thought."

CHAPTER XIII.

"Seek to Know"

1.

DISCUSSION OF artistic creation naturally led to the question of beauty and ugliness; and that in turn to what we call evil.

Gaelic made a distinction. However we may decide to define beauty, we are not justified in defining ugliness as merely the absence of beauty, as darkness is the absence of light. Ugliness is something to be considered of itself; and it is something to be dealt with as itself.

First of all, let us see what we know about beauty. The created object, whatever it is, consists of two things: the idea, or mold, and the material filler of the mold which makes the manifestation.

Now, says Gaelic, when the originating life force is so strong and abundant for the purpose that it not only molds and shapes its material into its form of expression, but has vitality beyond that and to spare, we have beauty. Per contra, when the life force is weak as compared to the stubbornness of the medium through which it pushes the pattern of itself, then beauty lacks. "It barely suffices to shadow itself forth in form," as Gaelic expresses the thought.

We can see the principle—which is of universal application —in the simple case of the man who has a certain sum of money with which to build. First of all he figures on the bare necessary structure. Only if then he has anything left over, does he think of the esthetics. The same applies also to his spiritual building. "If," says Gaelic, "he has spiritual capital enough, he can afford, and he delights in, the ornamentation of his structure. If he is straitened for funds, he erects a shed to contain merely his utilities."

Beauty results from an exuberance of the life-thing beyond the mere mechanical need of producing a manifestation.

2.

That principle is both universal and automatic. If there is abundance to the point of overflow, it cannot fail to produce beauty, whether, as is the case with the artist, beauty is a definite aim; or whether beauty seems to be a by-product of pure chance. We can discern it clearly in the processes of nature—the grass, the trees, the flowers, rocks and birds. They are all shadowings forth of the within-contained reality, outpourings of universal life. Their purpose in the whole scheme of nature is obviously utilitarian. It would not seem to matter whether they are beautiful or not. Nevertheless they are so, simply because they so abundantly embody their intention. We see also the same principle at work through less "natural" channels—once our attention is called to it.

For instance, says Gaelic, "Have you ever looked down the vista of a great cañon in a city; or have you stopped short in admiration of the serrated skyline of the piled up masses of man's habitations, milky with mist of fading light; and have you ever thought that this thing too is an upspringing from the Fountain of Life—exactly as the mobile hills of the forest are? And if you have, have you gone one step further and realized that this conglomerate idea of beauty and grandeur of the shadowing of basic life comes, not undiluted and direct from the pattern of the All-Consciousness, as do the trees in the forest—but has been condensed through the medium of man's creative power? So that, at a certain point in the creative process, man's personality has intervened, to gather to itself an attribute of the All-Consciousness that no other thing in nature has yet attained. And that is real creative power—to fashion from the raw material his own intention.

"But note this: man's intention in building the great city whose mass has so impressed you, has not been consciously the intention to produce this thing in the wholeness you have seen. He has erected his buildings according to his needs; he has grouped them according to his convenience;—he has no thought to the arrangement, to that general aspect that has made for beauty. But it was, it is beautiful. The reason is that in his reaching for and exercise of this creative power, which he alone in animated nature possesses, he has again joined forces with powers of which he has been unconscious. And if his city is really beautiful—not in detail, perhaps, but in effect —it is because in his creation have been infused the exuberant qualities—faith, enthusiasm, confidence, overflowing vitality. These, in spite of an ill-directed esthetic sense, in spite of the deterrent qualities that make for ugliness, have had their mysterious and invisible influence on the whole. Those influences are very subtle."

3.

So from one point of view ugliness is lack of beauty. It is also a deficiency of vitality. It is furthermore incompletion, says Gaelic. So considered, we can include for our discussion the concept of evil.

"Ugliness, disharmony—and evil—are such only because of their incompleteness. Rightly viewed, they are not finalities, *but fragments of material awaiting their more comprehensive inclusion in a larger pattern—the fragment is a curve of a larger beauty.*"

That "larger pattern" may be away out of our sight in the future of evolution. Or it may be within the compass of our present powers. It *can* be at least within the scope of our creative imagination, not by any "attempt at intellectual visualization, but by sympathetic faith. Not understanding, but trust. It may seem fantastic to you," said Gaelic, "nevertheless it is true, that if you enter this feeling you have accomplished a portion. Not perhaps the structure, but at least the scaffolding within which the structure will rise. So turn not your eyes away from those things which are misshapen in ugliness. They too cry out for the strengthening appeasement of appreciation. Here the appreciation must be commingled with what wisdom of creative understanding you may possess. A portion of that creative imagination you must strive to infuse into your attention, so that, even if you cannot see the completed lines, nor can imagine what they shall be, at least in the fragment before you you see the curve of a larger beauty. That is the basis of what we call tolerance. It is what is meant when you are told to resist not evil. Your reward is again more life; life in terms of expanding faith and confidence."

4.

"Therefore," Gaelic pursues the thought, "it is evident that what we might call a creation of disharmony can result in nothing eternal for the reason that it is merely incompletion; and incompletion cannot exist for a longer time than it takes for some other creative intelligence to tune in upon, and bring to manifestation, the complementing vibration, the added proportion, that will round out and complete the mold left by the other. This is true of what you might even be tempted to call malevolent and evil creations. They are extreme examples of incompleteness. But they are, nevertheless, fragments of a harmonious entirety. They are ugly because they are partial. They will endure because they are truly products of creative intelligence, but they will not endure in their present form. Completed, they will be seen as the lesser curves of a beautiful whole. They will be completed only by the fuller contribution of more advanced and more able creative imaginations."

That is one of the tasks of intelligence, to eliminate ugliness and evil. Not, Gaelic emphasizes, by suppression or destruction—not in the long run, at least. Rather by "utilization in a larger and more comprehensive pattern which must be creatively conceived. Complete elimination can come only with the final rounding out of the whole scheme. But each cast forward of perception accomplishes a partial elimination." And the bit our own lives are working upon and bringing to "rounded completion" may be also at the same time a fragment of a still greater pattern. So that our small individual accomplishment is "also releasing harmony which will add toward the perfection of a larger incompletion. These things are not partitioned each in its own narrow field of influence. The whole universe is a mutual back-and-forth, back-and-forth, helping and building, each assisting the other's completion but at the same time completing as well as it can its own. It is a beautiful woven interdependability. Every true spark you strike from out your own soul is a light that has not shone before and shall never be extinguished."

It all counts, says Gaelic. No occasion is so trivial that it cannot contain all opportunity for the spirit. No genuine striving is unimportant in the larger view. This too is a creative process; and here too all the steps of creative process are to be discerned. Even the "assuring the integrity of the mold by appreciation." Appreciation of what? Of the fragmentary incompletion of "evil" and ugliness, so that as clearly as we may we shall feel them indeed part of "the curve of a larger beauty." That realization in itself alone, Gaelic assures us, helps dispel the disharmony! It all counts.

"Each honest and vital effort, whether conscious or unconscious, toward beauty or that overflow that makes for beauty, is a constructive power. And the sum-total of those efforts, whether in a humble crocheted lamp mat, or in an attempt at stage effects in the theatre, or in an honest though pathetic effort at decorating a hotel lobby, or a flower over the flower-girl's ear—all make in the aggregate a formidable force of onword-pushing construction, which, even though scattered and comparatively unmarked, goes far to overbalance the spectacular disheartening destructions that get into the newspaper headlines and worry everybody with the idea that the country is going to the dogs.

"That is the justification that would comfort many a sad comedian, doubtful whether his silly bit of slap-stick fooling is worthy of a human on two legs. It's the aggregate. The Recording Angel idea is not so far off—with his debits and credits."

5.

I tell you these things, says Gaelic, that you may understand. "All great truths are simple. All great truths can be stated in a few words. All great truths must have poured within them all of man's knowledge and achievement before they can be understood.

"In simple days it was not necessary to understand truth. It was enough to feel it. But as self-awareness expands its circle, a necessity is born for understanding. And the more a man or a race demands to understand that which has heretofore been accepted on what you call faith, the wider, the more embracing, you may conclude, has become that circle of self-knowledge or complete self-awareness which is his measure. Do not be deceived by the cry that human beings should go back to a mere reliance on faith—when that statement implies that the faith is a narrow and specific faith in certain things. Man must always live by faith, but it is a faith in what is outside; a faith that knows that what has been in small shall forever continue to be in ever-larger. There are many faiths that man does not yet seek intellectually to understand—many. But what he feels, the things that now he is said to question, he does not really question—he seeks to comprehend. Because the penumbra of his self-awareness is gradually illuminating, as it extends outward, that which has lain in the shadow.

"Seek to know. And when in that conflict, that struggle, you unwittingly seek to grasp that which is not yours, the inevitable defeat will also strengthen in its repression for the outfling which must in due time take place. Seek to know."

CHAPTER XIV.

The Essential Simplicities of Religion

1.

SUCH IS the job we must tackle. Such is the catalogue of the tools and the aids we have or can expect in doing that job. Such are the methods by which the job is to be done. But there is for all of them one indispensable that is the atmosphere, so to speak, necessary for the breath of life. This is religion. But since the connotations encrusted over the term have so thickened through the long course of history, Gaelic for some time seemed to be dodging the whole issue. However, it was only the word he dodged.

What are you meaning when you say "religion"? he demanded. Are you talking about the numberless formalisms the race has evolved? The word "religion" may be used in either of two senses, said he. "There is the essence of religion, which is very simple and not diversely differentiated; and there is the outer appearance, which represents the essence to the individual. The first is always the same; the second is of almost infinite variety. The second never completely expresses the first, but to those who hold it in sincere belief it represents as much as is adequate. When it ceases to be adequate, it either is changed or, if retained, becomes not a medium of transmission of reality, but actually an insulation against it.

"These almost infinitely varied forms correspond in their variety to the variety of receptive apparatus. The variety of receptive apparatus is merely another reflection of the variety

149

to be found everywhere in nature, and comes into being from the same causes; that is to say, because of divergent developments through reaction to different environments, mental, physical and spiritual. Just as the fish and the eagle are both basically creatures embodying a common life force; nevertheless, owing to different evolutionary developments, one maintains his contact with the life force through one medium, water, and the other through a totally different medium, air.

"It is of course from this point of view self-evident that the exact outward form of any religion derives its whole importance from the degree to which it expresses the inner essence. But note that this importance derives (*i.e.*, communicates or transfers) only to that particular group with whose individual and personal receptivities these particular forms correspond. It is of less than no importance that to any other group of people this particular outward form expresses nothing whatever of the inner essence.

"Religion is a state of realization of certain simple essential things, an attitude of heart—" Here Gaelic broke off, expressing dissatisfaction over the wording. He explained that he really meant deeper fundamental currents; then went on. "It (religion) is a direction of currents brought about by belief in certain things which are facts, and therefore worthy of belief, only when viewed from the exact orientation point of the believer. From any other point of vision they may cease to be facts and become unworthy of credence.

"Take, for instance, a card. Looked at sideways it is a card. But suppose you look at it edgeways, and that furthermore you cannot be moved—that is your point of view—and no one moves the card. Then to you it is nothing but an edge. Another sees it sideways and says it is a card—of course it is a card! You see only an edge!

"Or suppose it is dark, and there is a piece of blue glass between you and a distant light. It would appear to you as a piece of blue glass, obviously. But from any point where the light was not directly behind the piece of glass it would appear black or non-existent. Religion is the same. Unless illuminated by being directly in line with the essential simplicities, it appears dark or non-existent."

The simple basic criterion of religious forms is whether or not they convey—*to the ones who practice them*—the basic simplicities which Gaelic called the essence. That, says Gaelic, is what differentiates them from superstition. Such conveyance, he adds, is "not necessarily to the mind, but to the inner sense currents of their lives." Nor need a religious form convey the whole meaning, the entire content of the essential simplicities; only as much of them "as has exact correspondence with both capacity and need."

"Therefore," he warned, "let no one deny authenticity to any form of religion whatever, no matter how crude, unless he is prepared to say that such a correspondence never has been or has ceased to be. Not unless he is prepared to say that he knows the inner workings of all minds. If he is to judge at all, he must know first of all what are the inner essential simplicities. He must decide whether outward forms convey those inner things to those minds. And finally he must be able to judge whether such transfusion equals the capacity. Since this can be done only by putting himself inside the skin of the other fellow, which is impossible, he is reduced to judging merely the results." Which implies a sort of omniscience. Better give the other fellow the benefit of the doubt, and allow him his religious forms as true and effective—for him.

Indeed, said Gaelic, we must beware of confining the idea of religion to defined and recognized creeds adhered to by the many. "A religion," said he, "may quite well be a religion of one, a relation of one man to reality. It is important to remember that. It is also important to remember that Religion with a capital R is one thing; but that religions are myriad."

In Religion, with a capital R, we must always find what Gaelic had called the Essential Simplicities. What are they? Gaelic next proceeded to define them. There proved to be but four.

2.

"The first of the Essential Simplicities," he began, "is a faith in continuity, in a progressing, expanding and continuing personality.

"I said *faith*, and not *belief*," he distinguished.

"This faith, in some form, is an absolute essential to anything that can be truly designated a religion under our definition. It is a tenet of belief in all formal religions, from the crude happy hunting grounds of the savage, to the complicated hereafters of civilized systems."

Someone brought up the question of the crass materialist who holds that man is merely a chemical compound, which reverts to its elements at death; who believes that death ends all. Is this a complete block? How much effect has it on his destiny? Such people are sincere enough—intellectually—Gaelic acknowledged. But he recalled our attention to his phrase—"not necessarily to the mind, but to the inner currents of their lives."

"There are indeed," he admitted, "a number of people who believe implicitly that there is no survival of personality after death; and an even greater number who are in an honest state of doubt as to that point. Nevertheless, the great majority of these people are possessed of true religion as we have defined it, and that religion does, in spite of themselves, contain its due faith in continuity.

"In their case very clearly you will get an illustration of what was said as to the real judgment being based upon results. These people will almost invariably be found actually to be living a life which is utterly devoid of any reasonable explanation unless its actions be referred to an ultimate faith in continuance. A life wholly devoid of that faith would be rationally one of opportunism solely. If death actually ended, wiped out the individual existence, and the fact was not merely believed, but actually and scientifically known, the individual would be mad not to live for the moment only, since the moment is certainly all there is. Duty, altruistic effort, the obligation to others—all those higher moral floriations that adorn the higher types—would be, not only useless, but silly. To adduce such considerations as that the individual acts as he does through 'self-respect,' or a 'desire to do the job,' or whatever you please, is beside the mark. Such qualities themselves owe their existence to the hidden faith that the personality continues. So, however vigorously held or strongly expressed is the belief in extinction, that belief is given the lie by the whole foundation-building aspect of the present life. It is an excellent example of the comparative unimportance of the form of *intellectual* belief, as contrasted with the trend and direction of the hidden life currents.

"So in examining any man's religion by the criteria of the essential simplicities, we must not examine his formulated belief, but should determine whether in essence his life is not logically and rationally conducted as one would conduct his life, did he avow a formalized belief in continuity."

3.

"The second Essential Simplicity which must, in some degree and in some form, be a part of Religion is the faith in the intelligence of and a purpose in cosmos.

"The outward translation of this is most diverse. It may be graduated from the head of a savage's hierarchy of lesser deities, through a partisan Jehovah, up to the widest pantheism or metaphysical concepts of which the highest minds are capable; but it must always be an intelligence of wider scope than is possessed by those who live under it; and it must have a purpose of some sort that extends beyond the comprehension of the believer.

"In the lower forms this translates itself merely in terms of a powerful superman with all man's attributes; and the purpose becomes sometimes almost wilful caprice. But the believer is always subject to the power, and must be carried along with and assist in the fulfillment of the purpose. In the higher forms oftentimes the intelligence translates itself into an orderly arrangement, subject to orderly laws; and while the ultimate purpose is itself obscure, the direction of the purpose is that of mechanical evolution. Nevertheless, even in the religion of such scientific materialists the essential is present. It is dim and small, and flickers in the wind of chill intellectual understanding, but it is still alight. The intelligent scheme is even here beyond the complete grasp, and the man is acknowledgedly in and subject to the current of mechanical evolution which represents to him the purpose."

4.

"The third and fourth of these Simplicities essential to religion are closely akin to one another. In the cruder aspects their exact significance is not so readily to be discerned as are those of the first two.

"It is necessary that man should realize his inner identity with his God.

"Among the primitive religions this is so diluted that it becomes a partisan or tribal affair. His God is as the head of a clan or family, dispensing reward or punishment as a father to his children, demanding obedience and loyalty, imposing rules and regulations, and even fighting tooth and nail with the gods of other peoples. In this respect he stands as the patriarchal head of a family, and the attenuated real-ization of man with this highest conception of which he is capable, is the same feeling of identity experienced by one who knows himself a member of a specific group.

"Truth to tell, almost every formal religion now widely held on earth, from that of the crudest savage to that of the supposedly highly civilized members of enlightened communities, is still of this type. In some this relationship has refined. The God no longer admits of rivals against whom to war, and a certain mystical communion sometimes draws the relationship a trifle closer. But actually, whatever the degree, the kind of identifying relationship is of the primitive sort; there is on one hand the Godhead, and on the other the multitude of children of that Godhead.

"Only recently and to a comparative few has come the beginning of conscious realization of this identity—has become known the conception of each living organism, each individual and separate consciousness, as actually part of, as actually sense-perceptions of, organs of, so to speak, manifestations of, awareness-mechanisms of, the Absolute, or All-Consciousness. Nevertheless, this conception, turned backward, obscured and diluted by lack of development, is an ingredient in all religions that have been.

"The fourth Simplicity is the necessity—to speak still in theological terms—of 'loving God.'

"The utter savage 'loves his God' only in the sense that he fears him, and desires favors. That is the first germ of any love; the desire for favors, and the wish for a friendly rather than an inimical attitude. As mankind goes on in development and his religious ideas also expand, this feeling is formalized into a command or an admonition that he *should* love his God—generally, in truth, with a penalty for not loving his God. And still later, in the higher forms of primitive religion which are but just in the process of passing, he actually does enter into a mystic communion with that something, still outside himself, which he looks up to as his Deity. Also, as a corollary which he imagines wholly a separate thing, he is admonished to love his neighbor. This counsel is particular only to the later and higher forms. But with the illumination which shall bring him to a full realization of his essential identity with his God, must come also the realization that in that respect he must share that unity with all created things; so that in obeying the old admonition to love his God, he will find that he is really admonished to cherish all living things that be, as though they were himself.

"This meaning, also again diluted and restricted by lesser development, has nevertheless been an ingredient of all religions that have been.

"These four are Religion. The growing understanding of them, the growing capacity for realization of them, is what raises, purifies, and will make universal unity in, religions. The outward forms of which, sometimes in one proportion, sometimes in another, sometimes but tricklingly, and at others almost with a flow, are only the measures of man's advancement in diversity. As he rounds the circle, these diversities, like all complexities in the cosmos, will resimplify into a perfect understanding, a more perfect realization of these four simple but fundamental things.

"My purpose in these little talks is two-fold," he ended. "First, to indicate the value of all sincerely conceived outward religions, no matter what their apparent inconsistencies, or even absurdities. Second, to call your attention to the fact that the most unlikely people—and classes of people—do possess true Religion, complete in all essential parts; and often in spite of themselves.

"The individual who does not possess a faith—not a *belief*—that comprises in some form or degree these essential simplicities that make religion, is stopped and stationary and a definitely destructive thing, which can hope from an orderly cosmic order scant toleration."

CHAPTER XV.

The Nature of God

1.

To WHICH of the innumerable conceptions of this God, into whose relationship we must enter, can we give credence? Is there a common denominator within all the varied beliefs? What is God? Are we privileged to ask that question of ourselves? Are we privileged to ask it of others?

Leaving ourselves and our present beliefs out of it for the moment, it would certainly seem at first glance that there is no denominator common to the multifold formulations of the god concept. The more detailed our anthropological studies the wider seems the diversity, whether we deal with savage fetishisms, or the Jehovah type of anthropomorphic monisms. In formulation there is no common denominator. If we are to find one, we must go back of formulation. In the end we find ourselves at what Gaelic might call another simplicity. It is this:

The nature of Godhood is that it is not understood.

That does not mean the statement can be turned inside out to say that whatever is inunderstandable is God, though that is a trend of simple superstition. But it does explain the successive historical abandonments of the old gods; the slow refinement, expansion of the god concepts. As fast as understanding overtook the gods they vanished. The savage worshipped, sincerely, the sun and the thunder until he learned their nature.

157

Then he had to seek further in other inexplicables for his containers of godhood. That is all these formulations are—containers. He grew out of his religious awe at the external processes of nature, and was forced to personify the psychological mysteries he found within himself. As long as they remained mysterious, they dwelt—for him—as a multitude of gods on Olympus, or Valhalla, or on the ultimate Planes. And so on in development to the later monisms.

Whatever the embodiments of godhood, they have been finite beings. The finite cosmos is so stupendous, what we understand of it is so small a proportion of that which our minds cannot even begin to grasp, that we the human race have not had to go outside it for the necessary containments of the awe and reverence and trust and faith without which godhood is an empty formula.

But in the rapid expansion of scientific thought we have lately begun to suspect, and to hope, that eventually we shall explore and understand everything in the material universe. We do not know an awful lot about it yet, but at least we are beginning to see how it might be done. We are sketching in the plan of intellectual understanding. We cannot grasp the actuality of light-years up into the millions, but we can talk about them; and by one or another device we are reaching farther and farther out into them. There is plenty in finite cosmos undiscovered, plenty we do not understand. But that incomprehensibility is not of the sort that can be fashioned into a concept of God, for we have now the faith that we are at least capable of understanding, and shall do so in due time.

In this manner we have slowly grown to apprehension that if there is to be a god for us it must be an infinite God. Infinity has come to be the only thing we realize that we are incapable of understanding. It has taken us a long time to get there, and yet the lesson is proposed to us in our first childhood when we look up into the sky and try to place a boundary to space—and wonder what is still beyond that wall! "Keep steadily in mind," says Gaelic, "that the Cosmos in its ultimate is inunderstandable by anything but itself."

We cannot understand the infinite, nevertheless we can postulate of it a few generalities. The Infinite must be inclusive. It must be all of everything—all there is, and in completion. The infinite God is all of consciousness; and we are told, consciousness is the one and only reality. In the infinite inclusion He is the ultimate and perfection of all and each of any attribute of consciousness. *All*-awareness, *all*-love, *all* wisdom, *all*-understanding, *all*-reality, *all* life and life force. And anything else of which we may become aware, and probably many other attributes of which we do not yet know.

2.

The aspect of the infinite in the finite is another matter. That is within our province of exploration, and within our powers of exploration either now or in the future. What Gaelic next has to say of our relationships deals with the infinite God, to be sure, but only of how we encounter Him in the finite. Our connection with the infinite is another matter, another mystery.

Within the finite we find the infinite has voluntarily self-limited itself to the laws by which finite creation exists. What the purpose may be we cannot even begin to guess, for it is part of the infinite scheme of things. Its immediate purpose—with which we are personally concerned—would seem to be the creation and the evolution of the individual consciousness. Expansion; growth; to perfect the individual. What his job or function may be after he has been perfected is out of bounds for our thinking. It need not begin to concern us for some eons to come.

Growth comes about by experience and by function. The created finite universe contains abundant material for both. It is also reliable for the purpose; its processes carry forward by dependable laws. Since the Source of everything is the infinite All-Consciousness, these laws have been conceived in that attribute of consciousness we name as wisdom. It must follow that there can never arise occasion for their transcendence or for their change, for they have been framed out of *all*-wisdom—they are completely wise. The plan of the universe is set and its processes will not be altered. We, the finite bits of All-Consciousness, can go forward in full faith and confidence that we shall carry on without interference. The rules of the game will not be changed.

Whatever aspect of the infinite God we may encounter in the finite, we shall find acting in accordance with and through these laws. That is what Gaelic means when he says that "within the finite the infinite has voluntarily self-limited itself." And, says he, the purpose is that of the rest of finite creation— expansion of consciousness and increasing awareness.

3.

God in the finite aspect, conditioned by the laws of that aspect, and God—the same All-Consciousness—as infinite and whole and all-inclusive brings us to the old ecclesiastical puzzle of Immanence and Transcendence. How visualize at once God as and in everything, and therefore one with everything; and God as transcending everything, which implies something not-himself to transcend? It is one of those fine-spun distinctions we do not really need to bother with; our job is learning to live, and this particular understanding is not necessary to that. This whole section can be skipped without harm to the argument. Possibly it is one of the inunderstandables that makes Godhood.

We can avoid a certain amount of confusion by the reflection that God as infinite includes all things, including His own self-limited aspect in the finite; pervades it; is part of itself. There is no partitioning off. Always when rigidity of thought or doctrine threatens our feeling of God in the finite cosmos wherein we dwell, we can slip out into the unknown for our comfort of mind.

Perhaps we shall have to do so if we follow Gaelic in his discussion. He asks us to confine ourselves for the moment to the aspect of God in the finite. There we must by the very nature of things postulate a dualism. One of the ends of consciousness, in the finite, is expansion, and that implies increasing awareness. So consciousness, in the finite, *must* contemplate dualism. For awareness we must have two things: the consciousness, and something of which to be aware. In other words, a duality; and that duality must carry into the finite aspect of God. Thus what Stephen in *Our Unseen Guest* so well proposed as a pluralistic monism. God in the finite is in that respect just like ourselves— He is a consciousness; he is aware; the objects of his awareness are outside the perceiving consciousness. That dualism is just like ours save in one subtle part. But that makes all the difference.

We did not create the duality; we are not ourselves that duality, only one part of it. God did create it; and is himself both parts of it.

As I said, this section can be skipped if only the reader will start the next with one acknowledgment—of God in the finite aspect as a dualism.

4.

All we need to go on, says Gaelic, is the concept that "the one member of the duality has that which is outside itself, to be sure, but only in the sense that it is contained by, surrounded by, comprised with the other member.

"Whether it is possible for you to gain a mental idea in this apparent contradiction of terms, I doubt," he confessed. "It is only necessary for you to gain the conception that within the finite the All-Conscious realizes its quality of 'I AM' by awareness of itself through response-contacts. And that the growing number and complexity of these response-contacts—which are experience—with their accompanying memories, make that growth toward perfect self-awareness which *seems* to be the end of the Cosmos within finity.

"In order to experience awareness-contacts, it is necessary to possess awareness-mechanisms—just as any created thing possesses the mechanism of awareness of its own peculiar type, needs or state of development. On the simple physical side, the lungs of the fish, and the lungs of the air-breathing creatures, are at once mechanisms of mechanical life, and of response to individual necessity and environment. The awareness-mechanisms of the All-Conscious, within finity, are what you call separated or segregated creations, whether the simplest or the most complex. Whatever any of these created things experiences in its impulse toward its own self-awareness, *is also an experience and a memory of the All-Conscious.*

"And as the memories of individuals actually and constructively enlarge and assure the body of expansion of the individual consciousness; so does the great aggregate of awareness-responses of all created things, becoming part of the All-Conscious possession, enlarge and self-assure the body and content of possession of the All-Conscious.

"I cannot hope to make you see clearly," confessed Gaelic. "You must be content with momentary half-guessed glimpses, as you see your own mountain peaks through the clouds. It is an inspirational picture I would draw for you rather than a plan.

"I must repeat one thing: you are capable of understanding only that to whose dimensions you have grown. Any creature is only so capable. You may feel intuitively, momentarily, something beyond, but when you would fashion it into a shape, that shape will be your own. You may think this is not of universal application, and perhaps your thought may stray to your doggie, and you may think that he is looking up knowledgedly to what is above and beyond him when he looks up to his human master as a visible god. As a matter of fact, to him you are only another of his kind, not a doggie but an animal, greater, more powerful, of larger possession than himself, but an animal. I would not be surprised if at times he imagines he possesses a greater wisdom."

5.

This is a big concept. Let us accept it at least as a working hypothesis until we follow Gaelic to his conclusions. Finite creations are the awareness-mechanisms of All-Consciousness in the finite.

In our own cases, individuals, our awareness-mechanisms are specialized. We feel with our tactile nerves; we taste and smell with our taste buds; we hear with our ears; we see with our eyes. So in the slow development of the evolution of All-Consciousness in the finite its multitudinous creatures have become awareness-mechanisms, each with its specialties, and its limits of response. When the amoeba was the most evolved thing on this planet, spirit in the finite* was self-aware only to the extent of an amoeba's self-awareness. In the course of eons we gained complexity, both in structure and in response. As far as we can tell, man, Homo sapiens, is about the top product to date in the visible physical universe we know. What may be outside that visibility is not the present concern. Better men, undoubtedly; but *men* in essential.

In our role of being awareness-mechanisms we stand for many things that we share with all creatures not so far along as we. But one quality is more or less unique to ourselves. At least, that quality has in us a stronger force or power of expression.

* We confine our illustration to the earth for the sake of clarity. Admitted it is possible—or likely—that somewhere they've done better!

"The human being, considered solely as an awareness-mechanism of the All-Conscious, is a delicate instrument of constantly increasing capability," said Gaelic. "And for an inscrutable reason of its own, *the All-Conscious has chosen to become best aware of Himself as to His power of free will through that mechanism.*"

All this is important enough for restatement. Just as the eyes and ears and other organs are the awareness-mechanisms of the individual, so is the individual the awareness-mechanism of the All-Consciousness in the finite.

6.

For purposes of pragmatic relationship then, says Gaelic, we can draw a kind of parallel to our own make-up, as human beings. We have our individual life, and we have also the numberless lesser, but distinct, lives of the cells that make up our body. These latter are separate entities; nevertheless, as to quality and kind, they partake of the nature of the greater entity of which they are part. They are, in a manner of speaking, *human;* their aggregate makes human flesh, and they are different from the cells of fish or tree or living rock.

The analogy that can be drawn is near the truth. "Let us," says Gaelic, "consider a larger body of consciousness of which human consciousness is a cell. This is probably almost inconceivable; but exercise your constructive imagination for a purpose. I speak partly literal truth and partly figurative symbolism when I ask you to consider what you know of the human race as a body of consciousness consisting of many individuals."

The race consciousness is evolving, improving. It began simply; it evolves to the more complex. In the process its cells gain a higher quality. They are no longer tree-cells; they have become fish-cells, so to speak, and in due time will still further refine. We, as humans, keep pace with the growth of our race. We are the sort of cells appropriate at the time. "The greater body," says Gaelic, "has passed through what we may call the rock period of absolute savagery. It has been passing through the hardly materialistic and mechanistic phase of its upward climb, and therefore men have been formed in outlook and perception of unchangeable materialistic and mechanistic outlook. As it refines, so do its constituent cells refine; and so *must* its constituent cells refine."

For bodily health, Gaelic continues, two things are necessary: the myriad of cells must function, and the central intelligence must be in proper charge. We are well aware of the former; if enough of the cells do not do their duty, we fall ill.

Fortunately they need not all be functioning properly, or we should be ill all the time. Some may fail, but we can still get along, possibly with health lowered, but well enough for progress. Those lazy cells continue to exist only because their fellows carry on harmonious working in sufficient majority to assure what we might call an average of health.

That is how it works in our individual physical bodies; it is true also of the larger body of consciousness. "If humanity in your present earth scheme is to continue healthy and alive, sufficient of its cells (ourselves) must function in accordance with the law of its being. Just as in the human body, if the cells live in harmony, the whole is healthy. So it is the duty of each individual to be healthy, in order to add to the weight of the majority. Only should a majority become unhealthy, disharmonious, would the proper-living individual be adversely affected, for then the whole entity is sick.

"I speak partly in parable," he warned. "It is impossible to be literal. I seek to give a picture."

7.

So much for the cells. How about the "greater entity" that has charge of and is manifested through the body these cells constitute?

We, as the greater entity of the aggregate of our body cells, are first of all concerned with their well-being. That is merely a matter of proper self-interest. "To the governing mind of the human body," says Gaelic, "the health of that body is an importance and a care. By governing mind I mean not only the thinking portion that moves the hand or places the foot upon an appointed path, but as well the submerged portion that carries on the mechanical processes of digestion, of circulation, that causes the heart to beat and the breath to intake with needed regularity. Given an injury to one member, or a disintegration of tissue, the intelligence hurries to the point the armies of white corpuscles which shall beat back the invading armies of infection and shall finally restore to wonted health the inhabitant cells of the invaded territory. You have recently become aware of the extent and the great strength of this supervision—more fully aware, but far from completely aware. Your various excursions into auto-suggestion, mental healing and all the other branches of the subject have given at least a hint of the reciprocal action toward maintaining health on the part of the larger entity in supplement to the contributions toward health made by the individual.

"There is," and now Gaelic closed with the parallel, "not too remote an analogy in the infinitely larger and more complex body of consciousness of which we are speaking. It is self-aware to an extent of which your self-awareness is but a feeble and flickering shadow. It is the source of what you have been pleased variously to identify as instinct, intuition, inspiration, cosmic knowledge, whatever label you please. It is the intelligence or consciousness which answers when your need cries out to it, of whatever kind. It is that which supplements, which fills out, which is aware of the deficiency and the desire of its own atoms. It is that which sends by one means or another the meed of healing wisdom, of urge to progress, of divine discontent; which complements the reaching of those atoms.

"Just as the human mind marshals its forces to repair disease, so this intelligence or consciousness floods toward the need of one or many of its creatures the influences most appropriate to the disharmony which has made itself manifest. In the human body—to go back to our original example—the reparatory forces are marshalled by the greater central consciousness only when through the nerves the report reaches that consciousness from the affected cells. On the purely voluntary side your mind instructs your hand to withdraw from the candle flame because your finger has reported through pain that its tissue is being destroyed, and begs for the assistance of a command to the muscles of the arm. Should you numb the nerves, or sever them, your finger would char unknown.

"In a similar way does the greater consciousness of which we speak exercise its intelligence in aid when it is apprised of need. But when it is not so apprised the soul may char unknown."

The nerve is severed.

CHAPTER XVI.

Prayer

1.

"THE MECHANISM of apprisal," says Gaelic, "has been variously defined. Some of the definitions are outworn; some are now in the process of being formulated. It has been called spiritual contact, permeability, porosity—you may search as you will for a word. I cannot find it for you in a sentence, but you have been told of it in many forms. But this you know: that with the birth of free will what has heretofore gone on automatically comes within your control. It is as though one had in hand a switch by which one turned the current of his need into contact with the greater consciousness of which he is part.

"In times past," continued Gaelic, "this openness of spirit has been called prayer."

The term has grown to have, in many minds, a taint of formalism, but it needs merely the freshening of understanding to pass current as bright as ever.

Prayer is not a demand for personal attention, it is not a petition for especial and detailed favor. It is opening wider the channel-through from the Source. From the Source everything derives, ranging from mere life and vitality to the highest aspiration. The channel is always open to at least the trickle necessary to sustain life. Cut off from it completely we perish; as the physical world would perish, were the sun to be blotted from the heavens. Indeed the sun parallel is so nearly exact that it will bear a considerable weight in analogy before breaking down.

We take from the Source whether or not we are conscious of it, or acknowledge it. The process is automatic. Were we to become completely impermeable we would cease to exist. Inherent in us is the guarantee of an assured dole. It is an allowance for bare subsistence; the irreducible minimum. It means penurious living, cellar-dwelling in dimness. Our instinct is to evolve a way of taking more abundantly, by some sort of effort of our own, to learn how to open the channel; how to step into full sunlight; how to receive more richly from the Source. In other words, to revert to Gaelic's picture, how to "apprise of need" lest we "char unknown." "In this sense," says Gaelic, "it is a turning of health-giving currents toward a needing part. By health-giving currents I mean figuratively all that is required of all that the greater consciousness contains; just as the blood is sent to a certain member of the body. If the member in need of something is receptive, it flows within him and accomplishes. If he is tight-bound in his tension of impermeability, it washes by him, and but a trickle enters in."

2.

Is that, then, prayer in fundamental? we asked. Is it merely a semi-mechanical device by means of which we hook ourselves up with higher power, and thereby get what we desire or can use? Assuming the proper intention, this sort of prayer seems legitimate enough. Or is it a spiritual realization? a communion; a state of being in which one comes into a mystical blending?

"If," replied Gaelic, "you mean the formal spoken thing called a prayer, its value is solely that it implies a certain effort and desire to come into contact with what you differentiate as spiritual forces. If you mean the actual feeling of communion or harmony or mystic contact which many people describe as the *state of prayer*, it is a realization.

"But," he qualified, "do not minimize the value of the sincere formal prayer, because that sort of effort and desire is necessary from your end, before what we have called our end can operate."

"A formal prayer may also be a state of prayer," observed one of us.

"A formal prayer may very successfully *induce* a state of prayer, but it is not the words of the formal prayer that bring realization. It is only that the words form an easy route," Gaelic corrected.

"The actuality, the essence of prayer—whether you call it that or not—" said Gaelic, "is a complete conscious unfoldment of self for the reception of the spiritual vivifying, healing and developing influence of spirit. Conscious unfoldment means necessarily a clear-eyed, honest, impersonal understanding of oneself."

Every time we give ourselves a candid appraisal and acknowledgment of lack, we strip off one layer of the film of insulation that makes us impervious. "Until," says Gaelic, "that film is removed, the germinating waters are prevented from their nourishment office. As to the intellectualization, there should be sufficient to produce complete manifestation. Sufficient and no more. The intellect is a tool for the specific and only purpose of complete manifestation."

Whatever formalism we may then evolve for ourselves— whether we call it induced receptivity, or altruistic extension, or any other term of psychist, occultist, spiritist, theologian or what have you—is our individual prayer; a device by which we reach a state of being. It is just that always—a device. Such artifices are necessary to most of us; and yet there will surely come a time when we can discard them, as we tear away temporary scaffoldings, and enter directly that inner stillness which is at once the condition and the assurance of receptivity.

3.

But while this is true, we are not on that account excluded from the warmth of personal response. We shall not get quite the sort of attention the old Jews thought they got from their Jehovah, but it will be attention and it will be personal.

We are back again at our fundamental paradox of the finite and the infinite, but we can at least know this: Since God is All-Consciousness—*all* of consciousness—it follows that whatever trait of consciousness we discern in ourselves must be a fragment of what is whole in All-Consciousness. That is, we find ourselves aware, capable of thought, instinctive, emotional, gay, sympathetic—any of the hundreds of attributes of conscious being. All these things are aspects of or attributes of our individual personal consciousness. But since they are parts of consciousness we shall find them in perfection, and in complete sum and proportion in All-Consciousness. *All* of awareness; *all*-understanding; *all*-gaiety; *all*-emotion, right down the line.

Now one of all the hundreds of things we recognize in ourselves as individual consciousness, is the sense of personality. That too is a property of consciousness. How then can we miss the very epitome of *all*-personality in our infinite God? All that is needed for the intimate relationship is the evocation by conscious recognition, and God in personality is there for our comfort as singly and as fully as our spiritual capacity can contain. No more.*

With this warmth of comfort we may enter the "state of prayer" which Gaelic describes as the essence. To this genuine personality we may address the prayer of petition on those occasions when specific help seems to us to be needed. If we have earned it, and the purpose is so served, we shall get help. Par-

* Expressed also in *Anchors to Windward.*

enthetically, it may not be what we think we need. But we can
ask in full trust and confidence.

Nor should we be disturbed by Gaelic's statement that
"within the finite God has chosen to limit himself, *in his finite
aspect,* to the Idea, the laws, of the finite." That fact does not
preclude aid; it merely prescribes aid within law. In other
words, no "miraculous intervention" in the usual sense of the
words. Miraculous interventions are unnecessary. Sometimes
the aid may be spectacular enough to seem to us miraculous
merely because we do not understand how the laws are ma-
nipulated to bring about the result. But then, we still know
very little even about the laws of physics. We ourselves are able
sometimes to extricate a very young child—or perhaps better,
an animal—from some emergency that seems to it hopeless.
The escape would look miraculous to it. But we merely used
our adult knowledge of natural law. An aviator gets into a
desperate jam with no way out. He offers a prayer; the "miracle"
happens; he escapes. He tells fervently that "his prayer was
answered," and he is quite right in that belief. He had done in
vain all he could with the natural laws at his command. Then
at the last split second some little "coincidental" twist to the
sequence of events "just happened." The twist was an entirely
natural operation of, say, a law of aerodynamics, but one quite
beyond his own control. It came into operation without rhyme
or reason, "with no reason to expect it," with "chances a million
to one against." Is it too far a cry to substitute the personal intervention in answer to prayer for the million to one blind
chance? If the intricate and infinite Purpose was so served, and
since the infinite Awareness was so apprised?

4.

In this contact, which we have named a state of prayer, we
are turning to the source of all things for the very life force

that enables us to survive. But the contact should not be one of grasping demand.

"The true type of seeking for spiritual contact," says Gaelic, "is of the type which does not *reach*, but which *expands to receive*. You are in contact if you open out your spirit. You do not reach for it, it is with you always. If you but reverently and whole-heartedly open your heart to it, you get it. The reaching is tension. The whole growing and reaching upward part of the human soul is toward its source, *but the turning toward the source is in open-hearted receptivity only.*"

That does not mean a blah passivity, nor even that state of monastic withdrawal so characteristic of medievalism. Even in receptivity we can make an active contribution. We can extend our capacity and our receptivity through the refinement of our spiritual substance, so to speak, to a greater permeability. We can enlarge our consciousness to greater inclusion. We can intensify our desire to greater magnetic attraction.

But that is more or less a matter of preparation, *before* the act. Our real function comes in *after* the act. We must utilize what we receive. We are in a way transformers of the current through. It is our obligation to formulate and launch into utilization. This is a flow-through from the Source, and in the passing on through some sort of manifestation it ultimately is rendered back to the Source again. The circulation is unchecked.

That is the natural and intended sequence, the rounding of the circle. That it has authenticity is attested by the distrust in which, deep down, instinctively, we hold the principle of barren "saintship" that retires to an ecstatic solitude of communion with God. In rare cases such a procedure may be legitimate, but only as specialization. Someone asked about the saints of history.

"They were normal, and had a place, to the extent to which they consciously functioned in the period of their times. To the extent to which they were seeking merely their soul's salvation or their own delight, they were not," replied Gaelic succinctly. "Grasping what is received and retaining it beyond a necessary formulating period before allowing it to take its course toward its proper recipients, is bad. It is most often for the purpose of adding to it the ornamental jimcrackery of personal egotism. Entire selflessness is as yet the rarest of virtues."

This type of barren communion is the more dangerous in that it sometimes results in a "certain kind of sincerely indulged religious ecstasy. What is received from divine contact is not passed on through its legitimate channels, but in solitude is reflected back toward its source under the mistaken idea that the emotional glow thereby excited somehow identifies the recipient with the source."

Gaelic called this a false ecstasy. But he begged us not to misunderstand. "I use the term," said he, "in the mystic sense of tingling high pleasure. But only he who carries his ecstasy eventually through the formulation period into manifestation of one sort or another, is functioning in the normal course. It might be so that one can receive from universal consciousness direct, but he cannot render back to universal consciousness *except through manifestation.* He cannot barrenly turn toward the source an emotion; however elevating and satisfactory that may seem.

"Anything normally functioning produces an emotion of pleasure; the pleasure is of a type and intensity according to the breadth and depth and cosmic significance of the function. The highest emotional content must be in the perfect functioning, that heart expansion which puts a man in contact with his source. The pleasure is legitimately enjoyed to its thrill of rapture *so long as it is a concomitant of function,* and does not become an end in itself. The proper action of any major function implies the proportionate functioning of any subordinate function. Can you not see, then, that a neglect of one or more lesser functions, because you get a pleasure in a larger function, immediately implies the pursuit of the pleasure for itself? It therefore becomes a perversion, as in the case of monastic ecstasy before mentioned."

"Wouldn't it be penurious to ask only for certain limited things in prayer?" asked Betty pertinently. "Shouldn't one reach out and take all possible aliments of spiritual growth like a healthy young animal?"

"You would become a terrible prig if you took only for the purpose of special manifestation," agreed Gaelic. "You receive what your instinct wishes, you enjoy what your enjoyment teaches, you give out what you have fully in your hands. If you are producing and manifesting in a constructive way, you will be utilizing in full that which comes to you from above. To try to get only that which you may expect self-consciously to pass on for the improvement of others is priggish and spiritually awful! If you were to pay too much attention to your spiritual processes, or your digestion, you would probably get a fine case of dyspepsia in either event. Use only sufficient intelligence in the one case or the other to avoid spiritual or gastronomical imbecilities."

CHAPTER XVII.

Paying the Price

1.

WE GROW indirectly by doing our job and living life. May we not also help directly? Can we not aid in developing ourselves by giving conscious thought, following systems, practicing regimens? There are plenty of the latter; they all promise marvellous results; and most of them insist, each for itself, that is the best, if not the only proper, way to live and act. Do they get results? Are they advisable?

Yes, they do get results, says Gaelic. Whether they are advisable is another matter.

First of all, irrespective of their individual merits, why do we want to use them? For their own sake, as an end? That is very bad; much like following some of the physical-culture advertisements into muscle-bound bodily futility, or doctrine for personal salvation into sterile monasticism. For the sake of developing, by their means, a tool for further action? That is better, but not conclusive.

Secondly, are the results of the right sort? Are they suitable to us? Do we deserve them at the present time, and by these means?

2.

The simplest approach to answers seemed to Gaelic through consideration of that very common belief that if you "hold the thought" long enough, and in the right way, you will get it, whatever it is. The practitioners of this system of painless acquisition can instance so many occasions when the result actually did follow the method that one's explanation has to be either a great many remarkable coincidences, or a great many unreliable witnesses—or liars. Neither of which is a particularly good explanation. Do these people actually get pianos and mink coats and ten-dollar bills and other material nick-of-time rescues in the occult fashion they urge?

By those who train for it, Gaelic admitted.

Why not train for it, then, we wanted to know. It sounds like a painless way to get things.

"For the simple reason," retorted Gaelic, *"that nothing can be acquired unless the price for it is paid."*

Learning how to "hold the thought" and then doing it sounds easier than most of the work we have to do to earn things, we argued. Assuming, of course, that this is a sure-fire system.

It may be easier, admitted Gaelic, but that is only the method. Payment is to come. "There are no gratuitous acquisitions," he insisted. "If a thing is acquired apparently without payment by the one demanding it, be certain that payment is made by somebody, or some group force, and the deferred price is charged against that one's credit."

And sometime or other "that one" is going to reimburse. To be sure he has paid no cash, but its price is still due. How much is it? When is it to be paid? How, and in what coinage? He does not know. He has bought a pig in a poke; and that, Gaelic points out, is never a wise thing to do.

"The simplest method for acquiring material possession for any purpose whatever is through the economic law that each clearly understands," Gaelic expressed this in his usual stately fashion. "The payment is made in the token you call money, which represents a well-understood and defined meed of effort, service or exchange. If you desire an object, you know exactly its price; and furthermore you know what the payment of that price means to you in these terms. So you may evaluate exactly its desirability as balanced against its price.

"Material possession may also be acquired by the invocation of more subtle laws than those of economics. The acquisition is certain to one, who thoroughly understands this law, and can inject into it enough dynamics for its operation. But the material object does not come into possession from a storehouse of gratuities. There must be expended for it a price. That price is not a fixed unit, as is the money token of the lesser economic law. It is a variable, depending on what coin you possess, and what coin you owe. There is also a dependence upon your purpose of investment, and its singleness. Each alloy of lesser purpose alters the coinage which must be paid. Only a Master is in a position to see as clearly and as accurately as does one operating under economic law the amount and kind of payment. As for the others who invoke law blindly, he is a foolish man who takes from the shelves careless and unknowing of price, of kind of payment, of time of payment, of rate of interest.

"That, in brief, is the danger of the knowledged invocation by rote of laws not understood, except in effects. Nothing comes into your hands but you are charged with its price. Know what you must pay before you strike the bargain. Know from whom, if anybody, you are borrowing your credit, and what repayment will be demanded of you. Aside from higher considerations, it is a grave foolishness to take, on such blind credit, that which may at least be worked for, if not obtained, by a comprehended law."

3.

So much for material acquisition by "occult" practices. How about spiritual acquisition? The cults and systems for spiritual development are as the leaves of the grass in number. Their teachers swarm, habited in robe and turban or in the ordinary garments of western civilization. They may be mysterious, and remote, and occult and ritualistic; or they may deal in plain words plainly used. They may promise merely personal growth and illumination, or possession of what amounts to outstanding magics. They call themselves religions, or sciences, or philosophies. Generally they are mutually exclusive; if one is right, all the others must be wrong. Nevertheless each is completely certain of itself. Furthermore, as far as the argument of logic is concerned, they sound reasonable.

That is for the sincere ones. And of course there are numberless perversions, imitations and synthetic fakes.

We cannot dismiss them with a shrug, but their multiplicity bewilders us. Perhaps we should not choose at all; but if we do, on what basis? And how about results—there seem to be results—are they good? Are they good for us? And how about those supernormal powers promised us as reward? Are they genuine? Are they desirable?

"It is perfectly possible to acquire powers beyond those you now possess or will gain in the ordinary course of your development," admitted Gaelic. "And these powers are not illusory. They can be used to produce certain effects. But such practices are perilously close to what might be called black magic."

At this point, however, Gaelic hastened to disclaim any deprecation or denial of what is genuine and orderly and constructive in those aspects of growth which are loosely grouped under the term "occult." The possession of such supernormal powers *may* indicate an advanced stage of development in the person of their possessor. But the latter has grown to them. He has not grabbed them by mechanically performing certain exercises, by rote. Gaelic made it clear that he was dealing only with "the accumulated fungus of misapprehension, unwise practice and extraneous matter" that has grown on the sound surface of the genuine. He is not talking about normal growth, but of forced growth.

Unfortunately it is possible to force growth by rote performance of many of these "occult" practices. And—as in the case of "holding the thought" for material belongings—to get results. A man can go through the motions and get something definite in the way of apparent development, and of unusual powers, sometimes very startling. But the catch is, says Gaelic, that such accomplishments, while real enough, have no endurance, no substance. "The apparent effects are of great magnitude," says he, "but the *final* effects are almost nothing. In the balance of nature a readjustment* will eventually take place that will bring about what would have been the original form. In the present scheme of things nothing actual has been accomplished." Why? Because, says Gaelic, the "magic," the occult practice, the formula-by-rote has precipitated into physical form no reality—or portion of reality. Such precipitation cannot be done by formula, but only "by a definite, normal and ordinary effort of the free will, acting seriatim, without gap, in the course of its regular progress in development." It may be that results attained by "occult" methods amount to something; but only if they are accomplished by someone using them, not as formulae, but as tools appropriate to the sort of person he is.

Any result, no matter how large, effected by learned rote is illusory and fleeting. No result, no matter how minute, produced by knowledged effect from within, but is permanent, whether in building up the performer or in adding to the sum total of the general progress. "The one," says Gaelic, "is of no substance. The other is as solid as the foundations of cosmos itself."

* Of the elements, disturbed by the "magic" from their normal arrangement in order to produce the effect.

4.

With all this understood, we persisted in our inquiry, how about X and Y? We were naming two friends who had plunged rather heavily in what they understood to be the practice of Yoga, and who claimed startling results therefrom. Are not they getting somewhere? Or are they actually harming themselves? Is the practice of Yoga, as taught and recommended in the West, likely to prove harmful?

That depends on what we mean by Yoga; who uses it; and for what purpose. Even pure and unperverted Yoga might develop one and utterly disorder another. Gaelic implied that generalization is impossible.

Nevertheless,we pointed out, there seems to be a belief, with many people, that it has general application.

"Very well," Gaelic agreed to the discussion. "It is a large subject. I will do my best. I must use figures of speech, and I must be permitted to change my figure without being accused of inconsistency."

There is nothing mysterious or supernatural about the evocation of unfamiliar powers and forces. You evoke the power of steam by building a fire, containing water, compressing the vapor. Then you have produced a force. You know exactly what you are doing, and why you do it. In similar fashion you go through a specific routine and produce what you call an occult force. The only difference is that you probably cannot follow the causes and effects. But you would have produced steam just as well if you had not known how the sequence worked out that way. In other words, it does not matter whether or not you know *why*. All that matters is that you *do*.

"Any fool," says Gaelic, "can evoke any natural force if he knows the more or less complicated circumstances necessary to call it into being."

But what he is going to do with it, and what it is going to do to him, is another matter. Especially what it is going to do to him. It is not unlikely to blow him sky-high, stated Gaelic categorically.

"If," he illustrated, "one develops a steam pressure of, say, five hundred pounds, he may usefully employ it in a machine adapted to that pressure; whereas, in a frailer structure adapted to one hundred pounds only, he would meet with disaster.

"Now there are certain degrees of power that are generated according to the strength of the machine. It is as though, when you had builded a mechanism capable of withstanding and using a hundred pounds of steam, the hundred pounds would be automatically generated and supplied in exact force and quantity by the mere fact of the machine's existence. And when you had constructed a machine of five hundred pounds' capacity, the pressure would also automatically and without intervention on your part accompany the mechanism. It is actually thus with the powers of the human entity. The machine in this case being the stable and eternal character or soul or spiritual body or degree of development or evolution to which he has attained, and the so-called psychic and other powers the steam pressure that automatically accompanies the machine.

"Now conceive that by a short cut, as you call it, your possessor of the hundred-pound machine should by artifice, and not by automatic means, raise his pressure to a hundred and fifty pounds, instead of building up the machine to that capacity and so acquiring it in the usual course. Without doubt the machine would run in an accelerated manner until something broke. In a broad and general way this is the difficulty with any forcing system aimed at an acceleration of personal evolution. It is not constructing a machine of added capacity; it is building an additional fire to raise the pressure. The attention is directed to the wrong end of the problem. Instead of saying, 'If I develop the capacity the powers will be supplied,' one says, 'If I develop the powers I can do more with the old machine.'

"The measure of capacity in the human machine is character, the soul capacity, the degree of evolution, the eternal body, whatever you will; and that, like the human body, is a complex thing. By lifting a heavy weight in mechanical manners you may develop enormous muscles; but if, at the same time, a corresponding nervous vitality is not also developed, the result is not a stronger man but a weaker man.

"To change the figure, it is possible by the application of water and artificial forcing methods to grow enormously and fairly in a very short season, but it is not possible to grow sturdily without the stiffening and stabilizing ingredient of time. There is no known system which, in a finite world conditioned by space and time, can successfully rid itself of that one ingredient. For it is an inextricable fibre of all finite things, and sooner or later its lack makes itself known by that absence of stability which indicates lack of fibre. The systems you speak of, and many others, are incomplete. If they possessed in themselves all the ingredients of evolutional development, instead of only a proportion, then indeed it might be possible by the very harmony of their completeness to accelerate the time ratio. But they do not contain all ingredients—only those which mechanically bring about the fair and watery fruit without the substance.

"I would change the figure again. It is important.

"Conceive of the human entity as a sphere composed of atoms of a certain size, these atoms representing all the diverse psychic characteristics of which mankind is composed. Now in the natural growth of this sphere, in expansion the atoms also increase *pari passu* in size, so that always the surface of the sphere remains, through the always intimate juxtaposition of these increasing atoms, unbroken.

"But conceive the sphere enlarged in its circumference of power by artificial methods rather than natural growth. The atoms of which it is composed have not enlarged in correspondence. How could they, since there is no growth, only an extension of the radii of power? And since this is so, they are no longer in juxtaposition on the surface, and your entity is open to whatever winds of destruction may be astir."

5.

The pace of evolution, on the average, so to speak, is reasonably near the same time ratio for all. Nevertheless historically, or perhaps contemporaneously, we all know exceptions: men who have moved faster than the rest, but whose growth has retained the solid fibre of which Gaelic speaks. The exception is only apparent. The process of growth has been the same.

"You have often seen a wee rain fall upon the seeded earth," Gaelic illustrated, "and the sun has shown, and once more the earth is dry and brown. And in the days later it has rained again, and like magic in a few hours the grasses have sprung from the hard brown earth, almost unnaturally; a forced growth, one might say. Yet beneath the hard surface the regular and orderly process of nature has been going on in due course, until the seed was developed to the very point of germination. Had not the second rain come so soon, naught would have happened until by the slower process of the moisture already accumulated the shoots had come more slowly forth. The second rain did not force a process, did not bring a development by a short cut, but merely furnished a favorable condition for the earlier unfolding of what was actually already complete. In this manner it may happen that conscious exercises, consciously performed, in a very few cases might bring a result; but it would be a result already achieved."

The real point of safety is, never to make acquisition of powers an end in itself. Aim for growth, and the powers will come of themselves, when they are appropriate. They are by-products of the greater end.

"One does not strive for such powers," says Gaelic. "They

come. They are a part of the pressure that comes with the machine. Build your machine. Let force, power, the ability to make rabbits come out of hats, take care of itself. When you have a rabbit machine, rabbits will be plentiful.

"You build your machine by building yourself. You build yourself by the exercise of decision, moment to moment. You get the materials for decision from what you have received. You receive in proportion to your receptivity. And thus you have chased your tail in a complete circle."

CHAPTER XVIII.

Pitfalls of Pride

GAELIC'S DISAPPROVAL of forcing development does not mean that he disbelieved in a reasonable amount of taking exercise. As an auxiliary to the automatic processes, in proper moderation, it may be of great help, whether in growing muscles or souls. We shall get them both, after a fashion, in the regular course of growth, but we can round them out to greater beauty and efficiency by a little intelligent gymnasium work.

"There is just one general admonition to those who would push ahead. Distrust the thing that seems over-elaborate. No genuine truth comes to mortal man until it appears to him simple. If it be not—to him—simple and beautifully in the order of the universe as he knows it through his own capacity, then either it is not a truth, or it is not a truth intended for him. Revelation accompanies due and natural growth of capacity. To him who receives it it appears, not a departure from the normal, beautiful, natural order of things, but an extension in kind. If it departs from that, it is suspect."

Not only does it appear simple, continues Gaelic, but it seems entirely natural that it should have come to him in the course of his everyday living. It does not mean to him that he has been "especially selected" to receive a great revelation or to declare a great truth to the world. Nor in his own conception of himself does it add to his stature above his fellow men.

Too often when a man gains insight he yields to just that

187

temptation. The illumination of what he has actually been about, in his daily life, for a long time flashes on him suddenly. Something, dazzling and valuable, has been revealed to him. He wants to share it. That is a good and proper impulse. It may also be a dangerous impulse. In his sharing he finds that the thing he has found works as well for others as for himself; the thing is not only true, but it may be made of general application. He desires mightily to bring about that application. This too is good and proper.

Such a beginning, often, grows from a group into a movement, a cult, a school. It may do an immense amount of good, with people to whom it is fitted, *unless* into it creeps what Gaelic at first called the "one sin," but which he corrected to the "one corrosive." Too often the very sincerity and success sidles slowly into exclusiveness, and that into intolerance. This is the *only* way; I am its *only* prophet!

"There are," says Gaelic, "a number of kinds of pride. Most of them—like physical pride—are merely amusing. Or—like mental pride—are merely annoying. But with spiritual pride you enter danger. It was of pride, and pride only, that Lucifer was said to have fallen."

No matter how worthy and workable the tenets of any system, no matter how authentic the revelation of it, the moment the element of pride enters, that moment it veers toward the left-hand path. It is at least diluted and damaged, if not suspect. The moment you, or I, or the other fellow, in our own thoughts begin to look upon ourselves as exalted to especial authority, that moment we too are veering dangerously toward the left-hand path.

"Anyone," says Gaelic, "who begins to set himself apart as differing, should begin to beware. We do not differ. The greatest of all those who have lived the earth life did not differ. Nor did He, nor will ever anyone, by sudden quirk or twist snatch aside the appointed offer. Nor will ever promise that such will be done, be true, or accomplished."

In proper perspective, even at our highest, we have not so very much of which to be proud.

"It might almost be said," observed Gaelic, "that we need our whole capacity and our best efforts just to keep from *hindering* progress by our inertias, our omissions and our hangings back!"

"One thing I can say," boasted an ardent seeker for spiritual grace, "I have finally succeeded in overcoming all pride. And," he added, "I'm proud of it!"

Apparently the only pride to which we are entitled is the paradoxical non-egoistic pride of doing our Job!

Epilogue

FROM TIME to time Gaelic drew word pictures which he specifically denied to be literal statements of fact. But he claimed they contained the "essence of fact," and were intended to be what he called "mind-stretching glimpses." Here is one of them, to end on:

"You have," he began, "stretching out in all directions from the place you stand, an immense universe of tremendous space, of something almost near emptiness. Here and there hundreds of thousands, millions, billions upon billions of miles apart, is a single small pinprick in immensity—something registering on your sense organism. These minute points of registration you name the constituents of your physical universe. All between them is empty space, space so wholly empty that you have had to make a grasp for understanding by postulating an ether— which has no registration on your physical mechanisms! This registration is comprised within narrow limits of vibrations, vibrations so attuned to the organs with which your body is provided that they become, through that attuning, the real objects in your cosmos.

"And now suppose yourself, by some magic of readjustment, to be attuned in your sense organs to a different scale of vibrations. Instantly the worlds and suns and stars and cloudy star-dust skies would be blotted into a black void of nothingness. From them would be conveyed to you no faint tremor of impingement to make you aware of their existence. But there would now flash before your reattunement galaxy upon galaxy of new worlds, new suns, new stars, and cloudy star-dust skies, occupying in the firmament pinpricks of space at those points where before had been only the empty void of ether.

"And still moving on, in still another attunement, this second universe in its turn would vanish and be no more; and in the vast and empty void more points of light would spell to your renewed senses more worlds.

"And so on, and on, and on, through the almost infinite reaches, until, in the nearest approach to omniscience possible in a finite cosmos, you would appreciate that in all the vastness of space is no empty point; that it is all One Thing, One Primordial Thing. And its manifestation in the complex is only as a man moves, and so sees new lights that were before obscured, and loses in obscurity lights that before have shone."

INDEX

Abstractions, 123
Acquisition:
  material, 178-179
  spiritual, 179-181, 185-186
Action, see Development
Adepts, 28
Advice, 97-98
Affinity, 49-50; see also Group, the
Aggression, 68-69
Aim, the, 31-32, 90, 185-186
All-Consciousness, see God
Ambition, 67
Appendix, the, 45-46
Appreciation, 125, 127-130, 139-140, 144, 145
Archangel and the Bird, the, 98-101
Artist, 113, 117-122, 123-125, 127, 129, 131, 136-137; see also Creation
Asceticism, 27-32, 174-175
Aspiration, 118-119
Attention, 107-108, 140
Avoidances, 31, 57, 68, 72-73, 109-111; see also Asceticism
Awareness, 78-80, 109, 161
  -mechanism, 80-82, 117, 162-164

Balance, 32, 47
Beauty, 86, 128-129, 141-144, 145; see also Appreciation
Betty, 21-23, 85-88
Bird, the, see Archangel and the Bird, the
Blundering, 43-44, 65, 66, 67, 77, 83, 95, 97

Capacity, 116, 183-184
Cells, health of the, 164-167
Cheerfulness, 103
Child, the:
  development of, 54, 76
  slum, 103-104
Circles of existence, 62-63, 65, 96
  enlargement of, 67, 69
  reaching beyond, 66-67
Communication:
  SEW'S technique of, 21-25
Compensation, 103, 109
  law of, 51, 96
Conflict, 61-64
  types of, 68-71
Consciousness, 62, 78-82
  body of, 166-167
  center of, 106-107
  in evolution, 77-78
  race, 164-165
Core of self, 33-34, 40, 109-110
Creation: 113, 115, 118
  artistic, 119-122, 135-139, 141
  medium of, 123, 129-130

Daily living, 28-29, 30-31
Death, 152-153
Decisions, 95-97, 186; see also Advice
Denial, 27, 28, 33; see also Asceticism
Deterioration, 97
Development, 56, 62, 103, 116
  by action, 41-42, 46, 67-68
  forced, 187

193